Just Stop Being Poor

For all the souls whose paths have crossed mind

-

the loved and the lost, the ones I have hurt,

and the ones who have hurt me

-

you have all shaped the pages that follow.

Contents

Acknowledgements

To my aunt Lily and my mother Jennifer, your unwavering support and belief in me have been my foundation. You took the risk of giving me the opportunity to further my studies in Australia, and for that, I am forever grateful.

To Benjamin Ong, my earliest investor and advisor, thank you for believing in me, seeing me as a son, and supporting me when Marsupium was just an idea. To Richard Kwan, thank you for guiding me through the early stages of entrepreneurship without ever asking for anything in return. You flew me across the world, opened my eyes to possibility, and stood by to watch me grow not only as a professional but as a person. To Tom & Sanja Hendrick, thank you for helping me navigate the complexities of business structure and legal matters with clarity and patience, and for sharing educational resources that once shaped Australia's state-wide financial education.

To Adelaide University's Thinclab startup ecosystem - thank you for providing opportunities to learn and grow alongside inspiring founders and mentors such as Zrinka Tokic, Shane Radbone, Jo C. Durant, Sean Grealy, Tabitha McFarlane, and Alex Cross.

To my friends, and the Marsupium team - your wisdom, encouragement, and faith in the mission have shaped this journey more than you know.

To the people who have hurt me, and to those I have hurt - you have been my greatest teachers. The lessons carved in pain became the seeds of transformation.

And finally, to you, the reader. Thank you for turning these pages and allowing me into your world. May these words serve as both a mirror and a compass on your journey.

Introduction: It’s Not What You Think

This book is not a lecture.

It’s not a finger pointed at your struggle, or a shallow slogan wrapped in arrogance. It’s not another how-to guide selling you overnight success. What you’re holding is a story of liberation - from within. A reorientation of how we understand wealth, energy, personal power, and the invisible narratives that quietly shape our lives.

If you’ve ever felt stuck, like you’ve done everything “right” and still can’t seem to get ahead - this book is for you. If you’ve ever looked at your bank account with shame, or chased a version of success that left you exhausted and self-doubting, hear this:

You are not broken. You are not behind. But you might be running an invisible pattern you never chose. And you’re not alone, ***most people are.***

You’ve likely seen someone who just seems to have it. They move through life with ease. They don’t force conversations. They don’t overthink their every step. Somehow, things line up for them. They land opportunities with little effort. People trust them, listen to them, follow them. There’s a kind of gravity around them.

It looks like luck. It feels like magic. But it’s not, it's ***alignment***.

They’re not trying to control life. They don’t need to. They’re attuned to themselves. And because of that, they’re attuned to others. Their energy isn't desperate or demanding. It's Calm. Confident. Clear.

And that's the shift this book is here to help you make.

Because here's what nobody teaches you growing up:

> ***The universe doesn't reward effort. It rewards energy.***

This is a hard truth to accept in a world obsessed with hustle. We're taught to grind, sacrifice, and burn ourselves out chasing external validation. That if we just want it bad enough, and work harder than everyone else, life will eventually reward us.

But what if it doesn't? What if effort alone was never the key?

Carl Jung once said:

> ***"Until you make the unconscious conscious, it will direct your life and you will call it fate."***

That's where the real work begins, not in doing more, but in seeing more. In understanding the subconscious loops, fears, and inherited beliefs that quietly run your life in the background.

Because most of us aren't making financial decisions from clarity, we're making them from trauma. From shame. From programming.

You've been told that money is about logic. But in truth, money is deeply emotional. It touches everything; your identity, your worth, your safety. Someone avoids investing in themselves not because it's irresponsible, but because they fear failure. Someone undercharges not because they're generous, but because they feel undeserving. Someone earns well but lives paycheck to paycheck - not because they lack discipline, but because deep down, holding money feels unsafe.

That's not a budgeting problem. That's a nervous system problem. That's a shadow.

Jung believed we all carry a "shadow self". The parts of ourselves we repress or deny. They don't disappear just because we ignore them. They live in the background, shaping how we think, react, and relate; to MONEY, to PEOPLE, to POWER. It's just the part of you, you have not acknowledged. It is part of you you learned to exile to survive. To become financially free, you must be willing to meet it.

We're going to go beyond surface-level strategies and dive into the subconscious terrain where your financial patterns were born. We're going to unearth the silent agreements you made with yourself. Some as far back as childhood, about what you're allowed to have, hold, or hope for.

Meet this shadow with honesty, with compassion and with curiosity.

Money without clarity creates chaos. You see it all the time, lottery winners who go broke within a few years. Professional athletes who earn millions, only to retire into bankruptcy. Celebrities, influencers, even entrepreneurs who hit financial peaks, only to lose it all.

WHY?

Because money amplifies what already exists within you. It makes your patterns louder.

Success without self-awareness becomes self-destruction.

Here's the paradox most people live inside:

The harder you try to fix something, the more it seems to fall apart.

The more you chase peace, the more chaos you invite.

The tighter you grip, the faster it slips away.

That's not failure. That's **resistance**.

You've been taught that tension equals progress. That if you just push harder, control more variables, micromanage every outcome, life will eventually bend in your favor.

But energy doesn't move through pressure. *It moves through* ***presence***.

Force creates friction. It builds walls where there should be space. It replaces flow with struggle. And without realizing it, you start standing in your own way.

No one teaches you how to breathe. How to trust. How to allow.

You're told to chase, but not how to pause. You're taught how to work, but never how to **align**.

The irony? The more you try to speed things up, the more life slows down.

But the moment you soften, when you stop clenching, stop grasping, movement returns.

That's when people show up. That's when the right ideas land. That's when clarity finds you, not because you forced it, but because you finally *stopped interfering*.

> **Letting go of force doesn't mean giving up. It means giving space.**

And in that space, everything shifts.

This is the difference between effort and energy. Between desperation and alignment. When you act from fear, you create resistance. But when you move from trust, you create momentum.

Trust doesn't mean doing nothing. It means doing from a place that isn't drowning in panic. It's showing up and saying: *I want this, but I don't need to force it.* That's the sweet spot. That's where things begin to flow.

Some of us were born into emotional safety. Others inherited anxiety, scarcity, and shame. That's not your fault. But it *is* your responsibility now, because no one is coming to fix it.

And here's the good news: you don't need fixing.

This book won't give you formulas or shortcuts. What it offers is more powerful—a **map**.

A way to stop repeating the same financial story. A way to stop chasing, gripping, forcing. A way to return to clarity.

The world isn't lacking in wealth. It's overflowing with abundance; opportunity, connection, creativity, and prosperity waiting to be received. But we can only receive to the extent that we're willing to see. The more we make the unconscious

conscious, the more space we create within ourselves to hold that abundance. The more we release fear, shame, and inherited beliefs, the more life begins to meet us with synchronicity, ease, and provision. You don't have to chase your worth. You just have to clear what's blocking it.

You just need to wake up. Life comes FROM you, not AT you.

From the moment you were born, you absorbed beliefs about what you're allowed to have, what's safe to receive, and what it means to be "worthy" of money. You didn't choose these beliefs - they were handed down. Formed through moments of rejection, pressure, disappointment, and unmet needs. Stored in your body. Etched into your decisions.

This book is about making the unconscious… conscious.

Money, to most, seems like a numbers game. Budget. Spreadsheets. Hustle harder. Spend less. But if that were the full story, we'd all be rich by now.

In these pages, we'll explore:

- The hidden emotional drivers that shape how we earn, spend, save, or sabotage
- How survival-based strategies are now keeping you stuck - and how to break free.
- The mindset shifts required to go from emotional scarcity to strategic wealth building.
- The lies society tells us about success
- The psychological ladder of wealth, and why internal safety must precede external gain.

We'll talk about the mental investments you make every day - in thoughts, habits, energy, and identity. We'll expose the attention economy, how your focus is being stolen, and how to reclaim it as your greatest asset. You'll learn why multitasking makes you poorer, and how small thoughts compound just like money does.

But most importantly, you'll learn to rewire your relationship with money - not from discipline, but from understanding.

This isn’t about effort.

It’s about energy.

Let’s realign yours.

Welcome to “JUST STOP BEING POOR”.

Chapter 1: The Poverty Mindset

Scarcity, Short-Term Thinking, Self-Sabotage

The poverty mindset has nothing to do with how much you have. It's the way of seeing the world - rooted in fear, lack, and limitation. You can earn six figures and still panic every time your card taps. You can grow up in luxury and still hoard, compare, or feel unworthy of abundance.

Why?

Because money is not just about logic - **It's about safety**.

At the core of this mindset is an emotional blueprint, often shaped during childhood, long before we ever earn a paycheck or swipe a card.

The roots of the Poverty Mindset: Childhood Attachment

Psychologists estimate that around 50% of people are securely attached, while the remaining 50% carry some form of insecure attachment: anxious, avoidant, or disorganised.

These attachment styles aren't just about romantic relationships - they shape our entire experience of the world, including how we relate to money.

Why Insecurely Attached Individuals are often "Richer" than Secure Ones?

While securely attached people have a healthy relationship with money, they're often less externally driven by it.

Meanwhile, people with insecure attachment styles (especially avoidant and anxious) are frequently found:

- In high-paying jobs
- Leading companies
- Driving themselves to accumulate wealth

...but often with less peace, more burnout, and more emotional disconnection from what they've built.

SECURE ATTACHMENT

Formed when caregivers are emotionally attuned, consistent, and validating. Securely attached people aren't less capable, they're simply less reactive. They don't chase money to feel whole, to prove something, or to feel in control. They tend to set healthy financial boundaries; They want financial freedom, but I won't burn out for it. They value stability over status. They rather feel safe than to be seen.

As adults, securely attached individuals often:

- Feel confident asking for support
- Believe they're worthy of love and abundance
- Handle setbacks with resilience
- More emotional regulation and joy in the process

Scarcity level: Low
Time Horizon: Long-term

Self-Sabotage Pattern: Minimal. They course-correct with compassion

ANXIOUS ATTACHMENT

Often results from inconsistent caregiving - sometimes warm, sometimes withdrawn. Anxiously attached people crave approval, admiration, and emotional security but they don't believe it's freely given. So they may chase high-income roles, overwork, or over-give financially to be needed or liked. Their self-worth is often tied to achievement, performance, or being the financial "hero".

As adults, anxiously attached individuals may:

- Overspend to gain approval. (e.g. Buying meals and drinks more frequently for friends)
- Undercharge due to fear of rejection
- Worry constantly about not having enough

Scarcity level: High
Time Horizon: Short-term ("I need this now before it's gone)
Self-Sabotage Pattern: Impulsive spending, guilt loops, or financial over-functioning in relationships.

AVOIDANT ATTACHMENT

Often stems from emotionally distant or overly strict parenting. Avoidantly attached individuals are wired to believe: "No one's coming to save me. I have to do it alone." Money becomes a control mechanism, a way to build safety without needing anyone. They often hyper-focus on building wealth, not because they love money, but because they fear dependence.

As adults, avoidantly attached individuals may:

- Hoard money but feel disconnected from it

- Struggle to ask for help or receive support
- Feel guilty enjoying wealth or success

Scarcity Level: High but internalised
Time Horizon: Mid to long term, but driven by protection, not growth
Self-Sabotage Pattern: Refusal to invest, fear of dependence, chronic under-spending despite having means.

These patterns are subtle but powerful. Insecurely attached individuals often accumulate more external wealth, but securely attached individuals tend to accumulate more internal peace. The strong difference between: "I need money to be safe" vs "I feel safe, so I build wealth from a grounded place."
They follow us into adulthood and quietly shape our relationship with success, security and self-worth.
Even for those who develop secure attachment, life is not fixed. We are fluid. Depending on the stressor or trigger, we might regress into older patterns - especially those carved deeply in childhood. A secure individual may become avoidant when emotionally overwhelmed or anxious when faced with loss or instability.

Carl Jung would describe this as the unconscious asserting itself - the shadow reemerging. We carry within us not only the adult we've become but also the child we were. When faced with uncertainty, fear, or vulnerability, the inner child - and the attachment wounds it carries often takes the wheel.

"The greatest burden a child must bear is the unlived life of the parents." - Carl Jung

This means that healing isn't a one-time transformation. It's a conscious, ongoing relationship with the self. Our goal isn't to eliminate fear, but to meet it with awareness. To move from reaction to reflection. From survival to sovereignty.

Your Shadow will Always be in the Room (Self Sabotaging Deeper Roots)

Beneath the polished version of ourselves - the one we post, present, and perform - lives a quieter, more powerful force: our shadow. These are the parts of us we've disowned. Formed in childhood, shaped by trauma, rejection, shame, or survival, they didn't vanish just because we outgrew them. They stayed, hidden beneath our ambition, our habits, our spending patterns.

And when it comes to money, they always find a way to speak.

A growing body of research in trauma-informed psychology and behavioural economics confirms the same truth:

> **We don't manage money with logic. We manage it with our history.**

Not every shadow listed will resonate with you - but some will. Like a truth that's been waiting to be named. Circle the top three that you feel most connected to. These are likely to be shaping your financial patterns in invisible ways. But also take note of the ones that don't feel personal. Because chances are, someone close to you - your partner, a colleague, a friend - carries them. Learning to recognise these shadows in others will sharpen your emotional intelligence. It will teach you how to navigate relationships with more clarity, compassion, and boundaries. Money isn't just personal, it's relational.

1. The Unworthy Shadow

Core Belief: "I am not enough"
This shadow whispers: You don't deserve ease. You have to earn every good thing. It leads to self-sabotage, overworking, undercharging, and a deep fear of receiving.

Daniel's Discounted Worth.

Daniel ran a creative agency in Melbourne. He built websites for small businesses, clean designs, fast delivery, decent SEO work. He'd been doing it for five years and had a loyal list of clients. But behind his confident branding and clean portfolio, Daniel carried an invisible weight. Every time he sent out a quote, his finger would hover over the keyboard.

$3000 felt too much. "Maybe I will make it $2500." he'd whisper to himself. *"They're a small business anyways.. I don't want to scare them off."*

But the truth was: they hadn't even asked.

In fact, just last month, a client responded to his $2500 quote with, *"That's surprisingly affordable."*

Instead of feeling proud, Daniel winced. He immediately replied, *"Well, I can also throw in a free logo redesign."*

He did not need to do that. They hadn't even asked for it. But it was instinct. He always felt he had to prove his value, not state it. Sometimes, he'd offer extras to justify his worth: "I'll add analytics, free hosting for the first year, unlimited revisions." He never asked himself why he did this. He just felt like enough was never enough.

<u>Moments That Require Financial and Mindset Literacy</u>

Daniel's story is full of seemingly small decisions that are actually rich with emotional and psychological patterns:

- **Quote hesitation**
  His pause before sending a quote wasn't strategy - it was self-doubt.

- **Unasked discounts**
  He lowered prices before clients pushed back. That wasn't generosity - it was preemptive devaluation.

- **Overdelivering without being asked**
  Adding free services wasn't value-added, it was value proving.

- **Avoidance of praise**
  He winced when someone called his rate affordable because deep down, he feared being seen as "too much" if he charged more.

- **Emotional flashbacks**
  His people-pleasing was rooted in childhood survival, learning to earn love, not expect it.

Mindset and Financial Concepts

Here are three core concepts underneath Daniel's behaviour:

a. **Financial Self-Worth Gap**
   This is the emotional distance between what you actually provide and what you believe you're worth. People with a large gap tend to undercharge, discount, or overdeliver out of fear of rejection, not a value mismatch.
   Daniel had five years of experience, results to show, and happy clients, but emotionally, he still felt like the little boy trying to earn praise. So, he priced from that place.

b. **Preemptive Discounting**
   A form of financial self-sabotage where we assume we'll be rejected or seen as greedy, so we shrink our ask before negotiation even begins. This often stems from internalised beliefs: "I'm not enough" or "They'll leave if I'm too expensive."
   His fear wasn't that the client would say no. It was that they'd think he was too much for asking. So he shrank the number before it even hit the inbox.

c. **Emotional Pricing**
   When your fees are dictated by fear, guilt, or approval-seeking-not by your skills, results, or market value. Emotional pricing creates burnout,

inconsistent income, and resentment, even when clients are happy.
He wasn't charging based on what the work was worth, he was charging based on how safe he felt asking.

Concepts That May be Relevant to You

- **The Freelancer**
  A designer quotes $500 for a logo, but right after the call, says "but I'm happy to go lower if that's too much." The client didn't object. The discount was insecurity, not strategy.

- **The Small Business Owner**
  A caterer consistently throws in a free bottle of wine. Even when not on the menu. She doesn't charge. She just wanted to not "look greedy".

- **The Employee**
  An employee doesn't negotiate their salary or ask for a raise, even though they've taken on double the workload. They tell themselves, "If I ask, they'll think I am ungrateful."

And that's the quiet tragedy of many entrepreneurs: "We don't just price our products. We price our wounds."

2. The Scarcity Shadow

Core Belief: "There's never enough"
This shadow doesn't care how much money is in your account. It's not about reality, it's about perception. Even in abundance, it feels unsafe. Leads to hoarding, chronic anxiety, or compulsive saving and under-spending.

Alina's Story: The Weight of "Just In Case"

Alina grew up watching her mother rinse out plastic takeaway containers and stash them under the sink. Not just a few, but drawers full. Her father kept spare wires, rubber bands, phone chargers from 2007. Their home was clean, but crowded. Every item had a purpose, even if that purpose hadn't arrived yet.

As a child, Alina didn't question it. As an adult, she couldn't escape it.

Now in her late 20s, she found herself doing the same. Saving every paper bag. Hesitating before throwing anything out. Stocking up on "Buy 2 Get 1 Free" deals, even when she didn't need the product. Her wardrobe was full. Her pantry was overflowing. But internally? She always felt a few steps away from disaster.

Alina wasn't stingy, she was scared.

She grew up hearing stories about relatives fleeing war with nothing but the clothes on their back. Her parents spoke of economic collapse like it could happen tomorrow. And so she learned that safety didn't come from having enough. It came from having more.

Even when her income grew, her fear stayed the same.

She had savings. But every time she spent, she panicked. Every time she threw something out, guilt followed. Every time she chose quality over quantity, her stomach knotted.

To her, abundance felt fragile. So she clung to clutter, not for joy, but for insurance.

<u>Moments That Require Financial & Mindset Literacy</u>

Alina's behaviours were subtle, but emotionally loaded:

- **Over-saving physical goods**
  Not because she needed them, but because letting go felt unsafe.

- **Fear-based buying**
  She didn't shop with intention. She shopped with "what if"

- **Low emotional ROI**
  Her things didn't bring joy, they brought anxiety masked as preparation.

- **Internalised fear from generational trauma**
  Safety was never modeled as emotional regulation. It was modeled as stockpiling.

Mindset and Financial Concepts

Here are three core concepts under Alina's Behaviour:

a. **Survival Conditioning**
   When your nervous system is wired around fear or instability, your relationship with resources becomes reactive. You don't trust the future, so you prepare for its collapse. Alina didn't need financial advice.

b. **Scarcity Thinking**
   The belief that there is never enough, not just of money, but of love, time, safety. It leads to hoarding time, energy, opportunities, and even relationships.

c. **Emotional Clutter**
   When physical items carry emotional weight. You don't hold on to the object, you hold on the identity, memory, or fear it represents.

Alina didn't need financial advice. She needed emotional safety.

This Might Look Like

- You overeat at buffets because you don't want to "miss out."

- You stay in jobs or friendships that drain you because "something is better than nothing."

- You fill your calendar just to feel productive, even when you're burnt out.

3. The Martyr Shadow

Core Belief: My value comes from suffering.
This shadow confuses exhaustion with worth.
Associates worth with suffering. Overworks, overgives, and resists wealth that comes without sacrifice.

Layla's Quiet Burnout

Layla was a freelance consultant based in Brisbane, working with nonprofits to help them improve community engagement. She was talented, deeply committed to social change, and always in demand.

She was also always exhausted.

Layla never turned down a project. She offered sliding scales even when she wasn't asked. If a client said, "We're on a tight budget," she'd say, "Don't worry. We will make it work," even when it means working nights and weekends.

Her inbox, full of "urgent" tasks. Her calendar? Booked out for months. Her body? Running on caffeine, stress, and four hours of sleep. When her friend asked her, " Why don't you take a week off?" Layla smiled but felt a pang of guilt. "I can't," she said. "They need me."

Deep down, Layla believed that if she rested, she would be letting people down. That if work felt easy, it was not valuable. That she had to earn her right to relax. She did not want to be seen as lazy. So she overdelivered. Over committed. Overfunctioned.

And she quietly resented how no one noticed she was drowning.

Moments That Require Financial & Mindset Literacy

Layla's pattern wasn't just overwork - it was internalised martyrdom:

- **Undercharging without being asked**
  She assumed her clients couldn't afford her rates, so she preemptively lowered them - out of guilt, not generosity.

- **Refusal to rest**
  She felt undeserving of time off unless she had "earned it" through suffering.

- **Overfunctioning in silence**
  She never communicated boundaries, because deep down, she feared being seen as selfish or unavailable.

- **Mistrust of ease**
  Any opportunity that felt too simple or highly paid triggered discomfort, she believed money had to come with struggle.

Mindset and Financial Concepts

a. **Martyr Conditioning**
   When we grow up around caregivers who model sacrifice as virtue (e.g., parents who never rested, constantly worked, or never put themselves first), we unconsciously learn:

"Love means giving everything - even if it breaks you."

Layla admired her mother, who worked two jobs and never complained. But now, she lived by the same invisible rule: "Rest is selfish."

b. **Guilt-Based Giving**
A psychological pattern where we give not from overflow, but from obligation. If it feels unsafe to receive without reciprocation - so we overgive, overfunction, and eventually, burn out.

Layla didn't feel proud when she helped. She felt safe - like she had proven her worth again.

c. **Value-Through-Struggle Belief**
This belief tied financial worth to emotional labor. If something doesn't feel hard enough, we assume it's not "earned". This is especially common in service-based work, where emotional labor is invisible but deeply draining.

Layla rejected ease - not because it was bad, but because she didn't feel worthy of it.

<u>This Might Look Like</u>

- **The Overgiver**
You offer free consultations, extra services, or discounts - without being asked. You're scared

they'll think you're greedy. But it's your body that's paying the price.

- **The Self-Employed Empath**
  You love helping people. But you mistake giving everything for making an impact. You're exhausted and underpaid, but afraid to scale or raise prices because "you might not be needed."

- **The Corporate Martyr**
  You stay late every night. Cover other people's slack. Refuse vacation days. You don't say no, even when your plate is full. You're the "go-to", but secretly, you wish someone would check in and say: "Are you okay?"

And that's the trap of the Martyr:
"You give everything hoping someone will finally say..
You've done enough."
But the only person who can say that - is YOU.

4. The Performer Shadow

Core Belief: If I don't impress, I'll be rejected.
This shadow ties self-worth to external success - grades, income, accolades, appearances. Overachieves to earn love, driven by fear of being ordinary or invisible. Often experiences burnout.

Julian's Golden Resume

Julian looked like he had it all.

A first-class honours graduate. Featured in Forbes 30 Under 30. Founder of a growing fintech startup. But Beneath the shine, Julian was cracking.

He hadn't slept properly in months. He secretly felt like a fraud. He was terrified of slowing down - not because he loved the grind, but because he feared what he might feel if he stopped.

Every milestone felt like a moving target:

- After the first $100k raise, he thought, "it's not enough."
- After launching the app, he thought, "it needs 10k users."
- After the feature in TechCrunch, he thought, "Why didn't they call me a visionary?"

Success was never success. It was just.. Temporary relief. He didn't celebrate.
He didn't rest. He just kept moving.

Julian's life was externally impressive, but internally unstable:

- **Endless striving**
  Every achievement was followed by a bigger, scarier goal. Not because he wanted more, but because he feared being irrelevant.

- **Avoidance of rest**
  Stillness felt dangerous - like the world might forget him.

- **Overinvestment in image**
  He poured time and money into branding, PR, optics.. While secretly ignoring his personal finances.

- **Inconsistent income**
  He underpriced services to "get the deal" or "build reputation," even though the clients were enterprise level.

<u>Mindset and Financial Concepts</u>

a. **Success-Driven Self-Worth**
   When identity is built around achievement, money becomes a scoreboard. But it's never enough - because the goal isn't wealth, it's validation.

   Julian wasn't building a business - he was building armor.

b. **Imposter Syndrome**
Despite external success, the Performer feels like a fraud. Every deal, award, or compliment is quickly discounted: "They're just being nice," "They don't know the real me," "This won't last."

Julian didn't believe he earned his success - so he kept chasing more to prove it.

c. **Avoidance Through Achievement**
Working hard becomes a socially accepted way to avoid vulnerability. When you're always busy, you never have to sit with the question: "Who am I without the accolades?"

The Performer hides their emptiness under full calendars.

<u>This Might Look Like</u>

- **The Serial Overachiever**
You finish one course and enroll in three more. You hit your financial goal and immediately raise the bar. You're exhausted, but terrified of being "average."

- **The Personal Brand Addict**
You spend more time curating your online image than managing your finances. You look successful - but deep down, you're afraid it's all just smoke and mirrors.

- **The Burnt-Out Prodigy**
  You were the "gifted kid" who always exceeded expectations. Now, you struggle with basic tasks unless there's someone watching or a reward involved.

And that's the illusion of The Performer:
"You try to earn love by being impressive - until you forget how to just be loved."
You don't have to perform to be seen.
You don't have to impress to be enough.

5. The Control Shadow

Core Belief: If I don't control everything, I'll be unsafe. This shadow believes safety comes from control. It micromanages outcomes, overplans for worst-case scenarios, and struggles to trust people. Hypervigilant. Lives in chronic tension.

Amira's Tight Grip

Amira ran a successful consultancy. She had three staff, fifty clients, and a calendar blocked to the minute. But while her clients admired her precision, her team lived in fear of making mistakes. Every email was reviewed twice. Every decision had to go through her. She called it "standards."

But underneath the professionalism was fear. In her personal life, she triple-checked bank balances. She tracked every cent. She couldn't rest until every light was off, every drawer was shut, every outcome predicted. Rest felt irresponsible. Delegation felt dangerous.

Even in therapy, she'd ask, "Give me a checklist to fix this."

Because control was her safety net - and letting go felt like dying.

<u>Moments That Require Financial & Mindset Literacy</u>

Amira's story is filled with actions rooted in fear, not strategy:

- **Micromanagement of staff**
  She didn't delegate out of fear of mistakes - not because the team was incapable.

- **Financial Rigidity**
  She tracked spending obsessively - not to budget wisely, but to calm her anxiety.

- **Obsessive planning**
  She rehearsed every scenario in her head - not to be prepared, but to feel safe.

- **Burnout**
  Her inability to let go led to chronic fatigue, irritability, and eventually disengagement.

<u>Mindset and Financial Concepts</u>

a. **Hypervigilant Nervous System**
   Control is often a trauma response. The nervous system stays on high alert, constantly scanning for danger. In financial life, this shows up as obsessive budgeting, decision paralysis, and over-researching.

   Amira wasn't budgeting - she was bracing.

b. **Scarcity of Trust**
   People with a Control Shadow often believe others will not show up, so they try to do everything themselves. This erodes team relationships, breeds resentment, and limits growth.

Her fear wasn't of failure. It was depending on someone else.

c. **Illusion of Certainty**
Control gives a temporary sense of power, but it's an illusion. Market's shift. Life surprises us. Obsessive control over finances, business, or relationships often leads to rigidity - not resilience.

Amira confused control with safety - but they're not the same.

<u>This Might Look Like</u>

- The Financial Micromanager
  You review your bank account five times a day. You can't relax until every cent is categorised. But instead of peace, you feel more anxious.

- The Solo Entrepreneur
  You do everything yourself - not because you love it, but because no one else does it "right." You burn out quietly, then blame yourself for not being "strong enough."

- The Delegation Avoider
  You avoid hiring, outsourcing, or trusting others. You'd rather do more than risk someone doing less. You tell yourself it's "efficient" - but deep down, it's fear.

You believe control keeps you safe - when it's actually what's keeping you stuck.
Trust isn't a reward. It's a practice.
And safety doesn't come from certainty.
It comes from capacity.

6. The Saboteur Shadow

Core Belief: Good things never last.
Uncomfortable with success of stability. Subconsciously creates chaos to return to familiar emotional states. Avoids long-term growth.

Ella's Patterned Escape

Ella had finally made it. After years of freelancing, surviving on odd jobs, and dodging overdue notices, she landed a full-time remote design role. The pay was solid. The benefits were generous. The team respected her. For the first time, she didn't have to worry about rent or skip groceries to cover bills.

But within three months, she felt… off.

She started missing deadlines. Pushed meetings around. Ghosted Slack messages. "I'm just not used to this stability," she joked to friends. But under the surface, the panic was louder.

"I don't belong here."
"It's only a matter of time before they find out I'm not good enough."
"If I mess it up first, at least I'm in control."

She didn't realise it yet, but Ella wasn't failing. She was fleeing.

She picked a fight with her manager after receiving constructive feedback. "They don't value my work." Two weeks later, she quit. No backup plan. No safety net. Just the old familiar chaos - anxiety, hustle, and instability.

Oddly enough, that felt safer than success.

<u>Moments That Require Financial & Mindset Literacy</u>

Ella's story might seem irrational on the surface, but it reflects deeply ingrained psychological patterns:

- **Discomfort and stability**
  She didn't trust the calm. Quietness felt like a setup, not a reward.

- **Success triggered panic**
  As soon as life felt "too good," she subconsciously tried to sabotage it. Stability felt unsafe because it was unfamiliar.

- **Self-fulfilling fear**
  Her fear of losing the job caused her to behave in ways that jeopardised it - thus proving her belief true: "Good things don't last."

- **Emotional familiarity over growth**

She returned to the chaos not because she wanted to fail - but because that's where her nervous system learned to survive.

Mindset and Financial Concepts

a. **Success Rejection Reflex**
Some people subconsciously reject success, stability, or abundance because it clashes with their identity or upbringing.

They don't believe they're "the type of person" who gets to live with ease.
So they unconsciously destroy the things they worked hard for.

b. **Emotional Homeostasis**
The nervous system craves what's familiar, not what's healthy. If your baseline was chaos or scarcity growing up, stability feels emotionally foreign.

Your body will sabotage "peace" to return to "normal."

c. **Sabotage as Self-Protection**
Ella's sabotage wasn't about laziness or incompetence. It was protection. If she failed first, she wouldn't have to face the deeper fear of being abandoned or exposed as "not enough."

This Might Look Like

- The entrepreneur who burns out every time the business gains momentum.
- The saver who finally builds up $5,000 and immediately splurges on something they don't need.
- The employee who lands a dream job, but "forgets" to show up for the first meeting.
- The partner who picks a fight when the relationship gets too close.

We don't fear failure. We fear unfamiliar success.
That's the paradox of the Saboteur Shadow.
To heal it, we don't need more discipline - we need more self safety.
Because the goal isn't to hold on tighter.
It's to teach your nervous system that peace is safe.
That joy doesn't have to be paid for with struggle.
That good things can last - if you let them.

7. The Orphan Shadow

Core Belief: I'm on my own.
Carries deep-rooted abandonment wounds. Refuses help. Associates independence with survival. Struggles to receive support or build trust.

Noah's Lone Climb

Noah built his business from scratch. No co-founder. No loans. No handouts. He took pride in doing it all himself - website, branding, marketing, bookkeeping.
"Don't worry, I'll figure it out," was practically his slogan.
People admired his grind.
But inside, Noah was exhausted.

When friends suggested he delegate, he'd snap

"It's fine. I don't want to owe anyone."

"No one ever shows up when it really matters anyway."

Investors offered to fund him, but he declined. Coaches offered support, but he ghosted them. Even when clients offered praise, Noah brushed it off. His subconscious believed that help came with strings. That leaning on others meant weakness. That the moment he let someone in, they'd disappear - just like they always had.

So he stayed on the mountain alone. Successful - but silently suffering.

<u>Moments That Require Financial & Mindset Literacy</u>

Noah's situation wasn't about pride. It was about protection. But his patterns were keeping him stuck:

- **Hyper-independence as trauma response**
  His refusal to delegate or accept help wasn't about confidence - it was a scar from past abandonment.

- **Rejecting ease**
  He turned down funding and coaching - not because they weren't helpful, but because trusting others felt dangerous.

- **Emotional isolation**
  Noah wasn't just doing the work alone. He was carrying the emotional burden alone too.

<u>Mindset and Financial Concepts</u>

a. **Hyper-Independence**
   Often rooted in childhood emotional neglect or abandonment. The orphan shadow assumes:
   "If I rely on someone, I'll get hurt."
   So they rely on no one. Even when support is available.

b. **Resource Hoarding**
   Orphan-minded individuals tend to save excessively, avoid collaborative ventures, or overwork. They see resources - money, energy, time - as things that must be earned alone and kept safe.

c. **Help Rejection Syndrome**
This is a subconscious pattern where receiving support triggers discomfort. Compliments are dismissed. Assistance is rejected. Not because it's unwanted - but because they don't trust it.

<u>This Might Look Like</u>

- The founder who never hires a team - even when it's hurting the business.
- The employee who works unpaid overtime because "asking for help means I'm not good enough."
- The partner who pulls away emotionally whenever things get close.
- The student who refuses tutoring or mentorship because "I'll figure it out on my own."

The Orphan doesn't want isolation. It wants protection. But the very armour that kept you safe as a child is keeping you small as an adult.

Healing the Orphan Shadow does not mean trusting everyone.

It means slowly teaching yourself that not everyone leaves. That some hands don't drop you.

That you're no longer alone.

8. The Guilt Shadow

Core Belief: Having more means others have less. Leads to self-sabotage, under-earning, over-giving, or rejecting wealth due to unconscious guilt. Believes abundance creates imbalance or takes from others.

Kayla's Quiet Sabotage

Kayla grew up in a working-class household. Her parents worked two jobs and still struggled to put food on the table. She remembered her dad skipping meals so she could eat. Money always came with tension - and sacrifice.

Now in her late twenties, Layla had finally made it. She was a successful copywriter, charging premium rates and booking out months in advance.

But every time she reached a new income milestone... She'd suddenly stop marketing. Or offer huge discounts. Or give away free coaching hours to clients who "couldn't afford her."

She told herself it was generosity. But deep down, it was guilt.

> *"Who am I to earn this much while others are still struggling?"*
>
> *"If I have more, am I taking from someone else?"*
>
> *"If I get too far ahead, will they resent me?"*

Layla didn't fear success - She felt ashamed of it.

Moments That Require Financial & Mindset Literacy

Beneath Layla's generosity were beliefs that limited her wealth and well-being:

- **Avoiding growth after hitting income goals**
  Not because she lacked drive - but because she associated more success with more guilt.

- **Over-giving to clients and friends**
  Discounting, free services, endless support - these were not marketing strategies. They were attempts to atone for having more.

- **Shame around visibility**
  She avoided sharing her wins online. Not out of humility, but because she did not want to trigger envy - or feel like she was "rubbing it in."

Mindset and Financial Concepts

a. **Wealth Guilt**
   This occurs when we internalise the belief that having more than others is morally wrong. It often stems from growing up in environments where money was scarce, or where people with wealth were seen as selfish or corrupt. Kayla's guilt came not from doing harm - but from feeling like she was no longer one of them.

b. **Empathic Guilt Loop**
   Highly empathetic people often absorb the emotional states of others. When they're doing

well, they feel responsible for those who aren't. This creates a subconscious cap on how much they allow themselves to earn, celebrate, or enjoy.

c. **Invisible Loyalty to Struggle**
Sometimes, people fear that success will disconnect them from their community or family.

> *"If I become wealthy, will they still relate to me?"*
> *"WIll they think I've changed?"*

So they stay close to pain because pain is familiar - even if it means holding themselves back.

<u>This Might Look Like</u>

- An entrepreneur who refuses to raise prices even though demand is high.
- A coach who gives endless unpaid support to clients that "need help."
- A daughter who subconsciously earns just enough - not more than what her parents ever did.
- A friend who splits the bill even when others offer to treat, just to "even things out."

Wealth does not require you to betray your roots.
It's okay to outgrow the struggle.
It's okay to feel safe, supported, and abundant.

You do not need to shrink yourself to stay connected. You do not need to suffer to belong.

Guilt is a sign of your empathy. But you are allowed to succeed without apology.

Let your abundance inspire - not atone.

9. The Fraud Shadow

Core Belief: If they really know me, they'd see I'm a fraud.
Driven by imposter syndrome, this shadow leads to perfectionism, over-preparation, or hiding. Even with credentials, experience, or external success, the person feels like they're faking it - and it's only a matter of time before they're "found out."

Elena's Quiet Panic

Elena had two degrees, five years of industry experience, and had just landed a contract with a top-tier agency. On paper, she looked unstoppable. But in her head, she was spiraling.

Every email she sent was rewritten twice. Every Zoom call left her overthinking for hours after.

And every time a client praised her work, she'd downplay it with,

"Oh, I just got lucky," or "It was not that hard."

Behind her poised presence was a gripping fear:
That one day, someone would realise she wasn't as smart, talented, or capable as she seemed.

So, she compensated.
She overworked. Triple-checked everything. Declined opportunities that stretched her - even ones she secretly wanted.

Because confidence felt dangerous. Visibility felt like exposure. And ease? That felt fraudulent.

<u>Moments That Require Financial & Mindset Literacy</u>

Elena's story might sound familiar if you've ever questioned your legitimacy despite having results. Here's what's really going on:

- **Minimising wins**
  She couldn't receive praise without downplaying it.
- **Undercharging or overdelivering**
  Her fees reflected her fear of being "caught," not her actual value.
- **Hesitating on bold opportunities**
  She avoided promotions or public speaking - not because she couldn't but because she feared she'd be exposed.

<u>Mindset and Financial Concepts</u>

a. **Imposter Syndrome**

This is the internal experience of believing you're not as competent as others perceive you to be. It disproportionately affects high achievers - especially women, people of colour, or anyone breaking into spaces where they've historically been excluded.

Elena didn't feel like a fraud because she was. She felt like a fraud because she'd internalised the message:

> *"You have to be twice as good to be seen as enough"*

b. **Success-Visibility Anxiety**
For some, success doesn't feel safe. More visibility means more scrutiny. And if you carry shame about being seen, your nervous system might sabotage opportunities for growth in order to feel emotionally "hidden."

That's why Elena avoided promotions. Not because she couldn't do the job - but because her body associated being seen with being shamed.

c. **Perfectionism as Protection**
Many who carry the fraud shadow seek perfection - not because they love excellence, but because they fear failure. They overprepare not to impress - but to avoid criticism.

But perfectionism isn't confidence. It's camouflage.

This Might Look Like

- A business owner delaying launching because their offer "isn't ready yet."
- A speaker declining panels because "they don't know enough."
- A writer who rewrites the same paragraph for three days instead of publishing.
- A consultant charging less "just in case" the client doesn't see the value.

You don't need to know everything to have something valuable to say. You don't need 10 more certifications to be allowed to take up space. You don't need to "earn" confidence.
You just need to stop waiting for permission.

Imposter syndrome shrinks in the presence of truth.

And the truth is:
You are already enough.
Even when you doubt yourself.
Even before you're perfect.
Even when you feel like a fraud.

10. The Rebel Shadow

Core Belief: Systems are corrupt. I don't follow rules.

This shadow rejects structure, consistency, or authority. Sabotage routines. Avoids budgeting, contracts, or financial planning out of fear that structure equals control. But in avoiding "the system," it often recreates chaos.

Jesse's Expensive Freedom

Jesse prided himself on being "different."

He didn't believe in traditional jobs, hated authority, and would never be caught using a spreadsheet.

> *"I'll never be one of them."*

Them meant: people with salaries, fixed routines, or long-term plans.

He freelanced when he wanted. Slept when he wanted. Lived day by day. On the surface, it looked like freedom. But when rent was due, Jesse would panic. When taxes came around, he'd ghost his accountant. When clients asked for a proper contract, he would stall or walk away.

> *"Too corporate"*

But underneath it all, Jesse was tired.

Tired of feast-or-famine income. Tired of not knowing if next month would be okay. Tired of pretending that chaos was exciting. Because somewhere deep down, he'd internalised a dangerous belief:

"Structure is the enemy. Control means I'm being controlled."

Moments That Require Financial & Mindset Literacy

- **Avoidance of Planning**
  Jesse avoided budgets, schedules, or long-term goals not because he couldn't, but because they felt like surrender.

- **Identity over stability**
  He tied his identity to being anti-system, even if it meant sabotaging financial growth.

- **False freedom**
  He confused unpredictability with freedom, without noticing that his freedom was costing his peace.

Mindset and Financial Concepts

a. **Anti-Authority Rebellion**
   If you grew up feeling powerless, controlled, or boxed in, you may associate rules with oppression. So in adulthood, anything resembling structure - budgets, contracts, routines - feels like a betrayal of your independence.

   But true power isn't avoiding structure - it's creating your own.

b. **Unconscious Sabotage of Stability**

The rebel often thrives in high-stakes urgency. Planning removes the adrenaline. Without chaos, they feel purposeless. So they unconsciously create instability to keep the nervous system activated.

Jesse didn't need chaos. He was just addicted to the rush of solving problems at the last minute.

c. **False Dichotomy Between Freedom and Responsibility**
Many rebels see structure and freedom as opposites. But in truth, structure is what sustains freedom. A budget isn't confinement - it's clarity. A contract isn't oppression - it's protection.

<u>This Might Look Like</u>

- Refusing to use budgeting apps or tools because it "feels restrictive."
- Walking away from a secure opportunity just to "prove you're not a sellout"
- Rejecting advice or mentorship, even when it could help.
- Undervaluing routine because spontaneity is seen as superior.

You don't need to give up freedom to build wealth. You just need to redefine what freedom actually means. Freedom without direction is chaos. Freedom with intention? That's power.

The rebel doesn't need to be tamed - They need to be trusted with a map they designed themselves.

11. The Rescuer Shadow

Core Belief: If I'm not needed, I'm not worthy.
This shadow finds self-worth in fixing, saving, or financially supporting others. It gives more than it has, overextends boundaries, and often confuses love with rescue. The rescuer sacrifices their own stability to prove their value.

Clara's Costly Compassion

Clara was known as the "dependable one."
If a friend was struggling, she'd help pay their bills.
If her partner had debt, she'd offer to cover it.
If her brother needed a loan-again-she'd send it, no questions asked.

> *"They need me,I can always figure myself out later."*

But later never came. Her own savings stayed empty. Her credit card balance kept rising. And even when she gave generously, a quiet ache followed.

> *"Why doesn't anyone do this for me?"*

Clara wasn't generous, she was seeking safety through being needed. If she stopped rescuing, she feared becoming invisible.

<u>Moments That Require Financial & Mindset Literacy</u>

- Overgiving as identity

Clara didn't just help - she had to help. Her self-worth was attached to being the provider.

- Self-neglect
  She postponed her own financial security in the name of loyalty and care.

- Unequal relationships
  Her giving was not always reciprocated. And when it wasn't, she felt abandoned.

<u>Mindset and Financial Concepts</u>

a. **Rescue as a Coping Mechanism**
   People with the Rescuer Shadow often grew up in chaotic households where they were "the strong one." They learned to soothe others' emotions to feel safe or valued.

   Now, they soothe others' financial stress - at the expense of their own.

b. **Codependency in Finances**
   Codependency isn't just emotional - it's financial. You may feel responsible for other people's outcomes. And when they struggle, you feel it's your duty to "fix" it, even when it drains your resources.

c. **Helper's Guilt**
   This is the guilt that arises when saying no, setting boundaries, or prioritizing your own needs. It's the internal voice that says,

"If I don't help. I'm selfish."
"If I don't give, I'm not a good person."

But giving that depletes you is not compassion.
It's a sacrifice for validation.

This Might Look Like

- Paying a partner's debt before clearing your own.
- Offering to cover dinner for friends, even when you're behind on rent.
- Feeling anxious if you can't "fix" someone else' problem.
- Becoming resentful over time, but blaming yourself for being "too sensitive"

You are allowed to care without rescuing.
You are allowed to say no without guilt.
And you are allowed to build your own safety before saving others.

You don't need to be the hero of everyone's story.
You just need to stop abandoning yourself in the process.
Love yourself please.

12. The Addict Shadow

Core Belief: I need this to feel okay.
This shadow chases relief through spending, stimulation, or control. It isn't about substances - it's about soothing discomfort. The Addict Shadow uses money as medicine: to numb, distract, or feel momentarily powerful.

Ethan's Empty Cart

Every Friday, Ethan clicked "Add to Cart." Sneakers. Gadgets. Coffee table books he never read. Packages would arrive Monday morning - and by Monday afternoon the rush was gone.

"I just needed something to look forward to"

After breakups, he shopped. After stress at work, he ordered food. When the shame set in, he promised,

"Next month I'll budget better."

But it wasn't about the things. It was about the feeling they gave him: Temporary dopamine. A sense of control. A brief escape from emptiness.

<u>Moments That Require Financial & Mindset Literacy</u>

- **Emotional Spending**
  Purchases were triggered by mood, not need.

- **Avoidance Behaviour**

Instead of processing emotions, Ethan escaped into consumption.

- **Shame-Reward Cycle**
  He'd overspend → feel guilt → binge again.

Mindset and Financial Concepts

a. **Money as Soothing**
   The Addict Shadow uses money like a mood stabilizer. It becomes the emotional pacifier - a way to fill voids or suppress discomfort.

b. **Impulse Control & Dopamine Loops**
   Dopamine is the brain's chemical. Anticipation of a purchase (not the item itself) gives a hit of pleasure. Addictive spending creates a loop: Craving → Action → Relief → Crash → Craving again.

c. **Budgeting Without Emotional Awareness Doesn't Work**
   If the core need is emotional - loneliness, sadness, lack of purpose - no spreadsheet can stop overspending. You have to meet the need, not just the symptom.

This Might Look Like

- Scrolling online stores when stressed or bored.
- Treating yourself after a bad day to "feel better" - but never really feeling better.
- Hiding purchases or feeling shame after shopping.

- Alternating between financial restriction and reckless splurging.

Your needs are valid. But relief shouldn't cost your peace. Dopamine fades. Debt stays. And healing doesn't come from another delivery - it comes from facing what you're trying to escape.

You don't need to quit joy.
You just need to stop outsourcing comfort to consumption.

13. The Perfectionist Shadow

Core Belief: If it's not perfect, I'll be punished or rejected.
This shadow links worth to flawless execution. It believes mistakes are dangerous and that only perfection earns safety, love, or success. The perfectionist delays action, overworks, and fears being seen as "not enough"

Sophia's Unpublished Genius

Sophia had been rewriting her course curriculum for six months. Not launching. Not sharing. Just.. tweaking.

> *"It's not ready yet. Once I fix the intro, and refine the workbook, and redo the logo… then I'll launch."*

But it was never ready. She'd watch others with half the skill post messy content - and go viral. She'd sigh, "I just can't put out something I'm not 100% proud of."

Deep down, it wasn't about pride. It was about fear.

If she launched and no one bought, that meant she failed. But if she never launched, her identity as an "undiscovered genius" remained safe.

So she stayed busy. Not productive - just busy.

Because in her mind, doing it "right" was more important than getting it done.

Moments That Require Financial & Mindset Literacy

- Chronic procrastination disguised as preparation.
- Over-investing in surface-level polish (branding, design) instead of core value.
- Avoiding launch due to fear of rejection, not strategy.
- Confusing perfection with professionalism.

Mindset and Financial Concepts

a. **Perfection as Protection**
Perfectionism is a trauma-informed defense mechanism. If you grew up in environments where mistakes were punished or love was conditional, perfection became a strategy to stay safe.

b. **Cost of Delay**
Waiting for perfection often costs opportunity. The longer Sophia delayed, the more potential clients found someone else. In the market, consistency beats polish.

c. **Imposter Syndrome in Disguise**
Perfectionism often hides deeper insecurities:
"I'm not good enough to be seen."
"If I'm criticised, I'll crumble."
The problem isn't skill - it's self trust.

This Might Look Like

- Endless twerking of your resume, website, or business plan.

- Spending hours perfecting on Instagram captions and never posting it.
- Saying, “I just have high standards” to avoid admitting fear.
- Holding yourself to expectations you’d never place on others.

Done is better than perfect. And progress only happens in motion. Your magic isn’t in flawlessness - it’s in courage. And your work can be valuable because it’s immaculate.

You don’t have to earn permission to start. You only have to let go of the fantasy that “one day” you’ll be ready.

The people who change the world aren’t the most perfect. They are the most willing.

14. The Avoidant Shadow

Core Belief: If I depend on others, I'll be hurt or let down.
This shadow avoids vulnerability by clinging to self-sufficiency. It hides behind control, emotional distance, and independence. In money, this often means hoarding, refusing support, and associating financial security with emotional safety - but never truly feeling safe.

Laura's Silent Fortress

Laura had always been the responsible one. She paid bills early. She saved up diligently. Her budget spreadsheet was immaculate.

But no one knew what she earned. No one knew how she felt about money. No one ever helped, because Laura never asked. She was proud of that.

"I don't need anyone, I've got this."
Until one year, when her business faced a downturn. She had savings, yes - but she was burning through them fast. Friends asked if she was okay. She smiled, "All good."

She stopped going out. Skipped rent one month, then two. When friends offered to support him, Laura ghosted them.

To her, receiving help seems like failure.
Admitting struggle felt like weakness.

She would rather suffer alone than feel indebted or exposed.

She was not selfish. She was scared of being judged. Of being pitied. Of being seen.

Moments That Require Financial & Mindset Literacy

- **Financial secrecy**
  Never sharing income, debt, or financial goals with anyone.

- **Refusing support**
  Turning down help even when drowning - emotionally or financially.

- **Hyper-independence**
  Equating self-worth with self-sufficiency.

- **Avoidance of collaboration**
  Preferring isolation over vulnerability in partnerships.

Mindset and Financial Concepts

a. **Hyper-Independence as Trauma Response**
   Avoidant behaviours often stem from past betrayals, emotional neglect, or unpredictability in childhood. Dependence felt unsafe. So now, needing nothing = feeling in control.

b. **Wealth Without Connection Feels Empty**

You can have money in the bank and still feel broke - because money without emotional support or relational safety doesn't create peace. Laura had savings, but not safety.

c. **Avoidance Costs Opportunities**
Avoiding hard conversations - like negotiating, fundraising, or asking for financial advice - leads to stagnation. Growth often requires collaboration.

<u>This Might Look Like</u>

- Keeping your financial life completely private - even from a partner.
- Declining help, then resenting others for not supporting you.
- Over-saving without ever allowing yourself to enjoy.
- Feeling guilt when resting or spending "just because"

Independence is strength. But interdependence is power. Your value isn't in doing everything alone - it's in knowing when to let others in.
Letting someone support you doesn't make you weak. It makes you human. And building wealth isn't just about money. It's about being able to say, "I need help," and knowing you'll be met with care - not shame.

Now that you've seen the shadows, you might feel exposed or even overwhelmed.

But that's okay.

This book is not here to shame you.
It's here to help you see clearly.

Because until you name these patterns, they'll continue to run silently in the background, controlling how you:

- Earn
- Spend
- Save
- Give
- Build
- **And most dangerously, how you see yourself**

The shadows you've just met aren't your enemies.
They're your earliest protectors - parts of you that learned how to survive in an unpredictable world. But what helped you survive may now be keeping you stuck. And that's not your fault. Most of these patterns were inherited. Learned. Absorbed before you had the power to choose.

But you have that power now.

Actional Steps: Rewiring Begins with Awareness

1. **Reviewing your transactions through a shadow lens.**

   Look at the last 3 months of transactions in your bank statement. Highlight ones that seem emotionally charged-impulsive spending, avoiding payments, or transactions you instantly regretted or over-justified.

Then reflect on each transaction using these questions:

- What was I feeling before, during, after?
- Which shadow may have influenced this?
- What need was I trying to meet?
- Whose voice or expectations was I reacting to?

Example 1	
Transaction	$220 impulse purchase at Zara after a stressful week.
Emotion	I felt invisible and underappreciated at work. Shopping gave me a quick sense of control and identity.
Shadow	The Performer - equating external image with internal worth.
Voice	"If you look good, people will respect you"

Example 2	
Transaction	Gifting $500 to a friend even though I was tight on savings.
Emotion	I did not want to seem stingy, even though I needed the money.
Shadow	The Martyr Shadow - believing love or acceptance must be bought

Voice	"If I don't help, they'll stop needing me."

2. **Observe Shadows in Others**

You might not carry every shadow, but you've likely witnessed them. Recognising shadows in your family, friends and community can help you understand:

- Where your beliefs came from
- What financial dynamics you absorbed by osmosis
- How to stop personalising someone else's pain or projection

Example 1: Your Mother (The Scarcity Shadow)
Clipped every coupon, obsessed over discounts, even when it wasn't necessary.
You inherited a belief that money is always on the verge of running out - even when it's there.

Example 1: Your Friend (The Control Shadow)
Every time we go out, she calculates the bill to the exact cent. There's no room for generosity or grace.
If you are not careful, people will take advantage of you.

The moment you bring awareness to these hidden patterns - when you stop blaming your bank balance and start listening to your emotional blueprint, you reclaim the pen. You stop running the script you were handed and start writing your own.

This is where your real financial journey begins.

Because true wealth isn't built from force. It's built from clarity. From knowing what you're carrying, why you're carrying it, and what you're ready to let go of.

As we move into the next chapter, we'll begin to shift from survival thinking into strategic growth. We'll explore how every choice you make, what you focus on, where you spend your energy, and how you frame your thoughts, is a mental investment. And just like compound interest, those investments multiply over time.

This is the part where you stop leaking energy into your past... And begin investing it in your future.

Chapter 2: The Mental Investment Strategy

Attention, Delayed Gratification, Compound Thinking

You've met your shadow. You've seen how your childhood, attachments, and emotional wounds shape your financial behaviours. But now, we turn the page - not to escape the past, but to invest in your future.

Chapter 1 was about **awareness**, Chapter 2 is about **agency**.

Because here's the truth:

> *Every decision is a mental investment.*
> *Every thought, belief, habit, and pattern compounds - for better or worse.*

You don't need to be a millionaire to start investing. You've been investing all along.

> *In your* ***thoughts.***
> *In your* ***time.***
> *In your* ***energy.***
> *In your* ***focus.***

The question is? What kind of return has your mind been giving you?

Attention

Every Thought is a Currency

Let's redefine wealth. Not just in dollars - but in attention. Your greatest wealth-building tools are not spreadsheets and budgeting plans. It's between your ears: **your mind.**

Every day, you're spending mental currency. Your **time**. Your **energy**. Your **focus**. And in the world we live in, those resources are constantly under siege. We are bombarded with distractions engineered to hijack the brain's reward system. Quick dopamine hits from TikTok, Instagram, YouTube shorts.

> *"Double it and give it to the next person."*
> *"English or Spanish?"*

Endless reels. Clickbait headlines. Pornography. Get-rich-quick schemes that promise the world, and cost you your clarity.

Most people do not realise this, but they are not in control of their attention. They are being controlled by the content creators who understand psychology better than they do.

> ***If you do not program your own mind, someone else will.***

We are seduced by external stimuli because it is easier than facing internal discomfort. It's easier to scroll than to sit in silence. Easier to follow than to question. Easier to be entertained than to be intentional.

And as long as we allow others to dictate our focus, we will continue to hand over our future in exchange for momentary pleasure.

But this isn't about productivity or success. This is about **regret.**

In her work as a palliative care nurse, Bronnie Ware documented the most common regrets of people on their deathbeds. She sat with hundreds of patients in their final days - and what surfaced was not a wish for more money or recognition, but a longing for alignment, courage and connection.

Here are the Top 5 Regrets of the Dying:

1. "I wish I had the courage to live a life true to myself, not the life others expected of me."

2. "I wish I hadn't worked so hard."

3. "I wish I'd had the courage to express my feelings."

4. "I wish I had stayed in touch with my friends."

5. "I wish I had let myself be happier."

Let that sink in for a bit. Not one of those regrets is about failing to please others. They're all about abandoning the self. Living for validation. Suppressing emotion. Overworking. Disconnecting from joy.

These regrets are the real cost of mental misinvestment.

*We trade our **authenticity for approval.***

We trade our ***time for productivity.***
We trade our ***peace for performance.***
We trade our ***attention for distraction.***

And by the time we realise it, the account is nearly empty.

Wealth is not about accumulation. It's about alignment.
And without regular deposits into your mind - your clarity, your values, your intention -
You'll always be rich in regret and poor in fulfillment.

Now that we understand the emotional cost of distraction, let's turn to history - and explore how power structures have always known how to exploit our attention and emotions for control.

The Colosseum Wasn't Just Entertainment

History teaches us this is not new.

The Roman Empire did not build the Colosseum just for sport - they built it for **control.**

Known as "bread and circuses", the games were designed to distract the public from rising inequality, political instability, and civil unrest. By offering free food and violent spectacle, the ruling class pacified the masses. **Distraction became a tool of domination.**

But there was a deeper strategy behind it too:
The Colosseum wasn't just entertainment - it was **propaganda.** A symbol of power. A way for the Flavian Dynasty to restore

faith in the empire, legitimise their rule, and subtly remind the population who is in charge.

> *Keep them fed. Keep them entertained. Keep them quiet.*

The parallels to today's attention economy are no coincidence. Modern bread and circuses come in **pixels, pings, and dopamine loops** - the outcome is the same:

Distraction delays revolution.
The quiet, personal rebellion to take control of your own life.

Delayed Gratification

Climbing the Wealth Dynamic Ladder

Unlike Maslow's Pyramid, which assumes we climb step-by-step through our needs, the Wealth Dynamics Diamond reflects a deeper truth: our journey toward wealth isn't linear - it's layered, cyclical, and multidimensional.

Each level of wealth isn't just about how much you earn - it's how you think, where you place your energy, and what you're willing to delay for something greater.

The Wealth Dynamic Diamond

It’s about evolving through eight energetic levels that reflect not just income, but your mindset, habits, attention, and how well you delay gratification in service of something bigger.

Here’s the structure:

Level 1: The Victim - Trapped in helplessness, debt, or survival paralysis

Level 2: The Survival - Living paycheck to paycheck, reactive and strained

Level 3: The Worker - Earning consistently, but stuck in time-for-money

Level 4: The Player - Creating income streams through skill and initiative

Level 5: The Builder - Scaling a business, building systems, testing leverage

Level 6: The Team Composer - Delegating, leading, separating time from income

Level 7: The Sovereign - Time and location freedom, strategic ownership

Level 8: The Visionary - Impact beyond the self; leading movements, not just teams

The shape of the Diamond is intentional. The base and tip are narrow, representing the minority who are either stuck in complete disempowerment or operating at the highest levels of freedom and impact.

The middle is widest - because that's where most people live. Busy, building, experimenting, stuck somewhere between survival and scale.

But here's the key: Every level reflects not just financial situation, but a mental investment strategy.

> *Where is your time going?*
> *Where is your energy leaking?*
> *What are you giving your attention to?*
> *What are you willing to delay now, to grow into something greater?*

We all dream of becoming a millionaire. But if you sit down and do the math - your monthly cost of living, how much you can realistically save each month - you'll quickly see that the 9-5 job alone won't get you there anytime soon. At best, it takes decades.

That's why climbing the wealth dynamic diamond is not just "earning more" in the traditional sense. It's about producing - finding ways to create value, generate income streams, and shift your energy away from just trading time for money. Whether that's starting a small side hustle, building systems that save you money, or investing early, wealth requires a mindset shift: from consumer to producer.

You do not move up by hustling harder. You move up by investing better **Mentally. Emotionally. Energetically.**

Level 1: The Victim

Core Belief: "Nothing I do will make a difference."
Mental ROI: Negative. Thoughts and energy reinforce powerlessness.
Emotional Landscape: Shame, despair, exhaustion, fear, self-blame.

a. Overview

Level 1 represents individuals who feel completely disempowered in their financial life. This isn't just about low income - it's about a deep sense of hopelessness, often shaped by repeated setbacks, trauma, or prolonged instability. At this level, survival itself can feel uncertain, and personal agency feels out of reach.

The term "Victim" here does not imply weakness of failure. Rather, it reflects a psychological state in which a person has internalised the belief that external circumstances control their outcomes. These individuals are not lazy - they are often mentally and emotionally exhausted from trying without seeing results.

b. Common Thought Patterns

People operating at Level 1 tend to carry thoughts such as:

- "No matter what I do, nothing changes."
- "The system is rigged against people like me."

- “I’ve failed too many times. What’s the point in trying again?”

- “Everyone else has something I don’t - luck, support, opportunity.”

These beliefs are often reinforced by past experiences: Job loss, unstable housing, systemic inequality, or lack of support in childhood or adulthood. Over time, these experiences compound into a learned helplessness - where doing less feels safer than risking disappointment again.

c. The Illusion of Inactivity

From the outside , it may appear that someone at this level is disengaged or unmotivated. In reality, many are mentally overwhelmed - constantly cycling through fear, regret, or survival-mode decision-making.

Their time and energy may be consumed by:

- Ruminating on past failures
- Worrying about basic needs
- Avoiding tasks that feel too emotionally taxing
- Comparing themselves to others and feeling stuck

The result is a type of emotional burnout that looks like inactivity, but is actually the body and mind trying to preserve what little capacity remains.

d. How Time, Energy, and Attention Are Spent

Resource	Typical Use at Level 1
Time	Spent avoiding triggers, managing immediate crises, or numbing discomfort.
Energy	Drained by overthinking, shame, fear of failure, and self-criticism.
Attention	Focused on survival, perceived limitations, and past regrets.

The return on these investments is low - not because the person is incapable, but because the system they are operating within (both internal and external) is misaligned with growth.

e. The Turning Point: From Hopelessness to Small Wins

Progress at this level does not begin with radical change. It begins with credibility-building moments - small wins that prove to the brain that change is possible.

Some examples include:

- Completing a short task (e.g. updating a resume, calling a service provider)
- Earning a small amount of money through a side hustle or gig
- Setting a clear boundary with someone draining your energy

- Asking for help from a mentor, friend or professional

These actions are not just tasks - they are **emotional milestones** that begin to rebuild trust in one's ability to make a difference.

f. Delayed gratification Strategy for Level 1

At this level, the idea of long-term planning can feel overwhelming. So the delayed gratification principle should be applied on a micro scale.

> *"What can I do today that my future self will thank me for tomorrow?"*
> *E.g.*
> - *Going for a walk instead of spiraling online*
> - *Preparing one simple meal instead of ordering out*
> - *Spending 30 minutes learning a new skill instead of numbing with entertainment*

The goal isn't transformation. It's traction.

g. Mental Investment Reframe

Default Thought: "It's not worth trying."
Growth-Oriented Reframe: "Even one step forward is better than staying still."

Default Thought: "Other people have it easier."

Growth-Oriented Reframe: “I can’t change where I started, but I can influence where I go next.”

-

Breaking out of Level 1 is difficult - not because of a lack of intelligence or effort, but because it **requires believing in yourself before you have evidence**. It requires choosing **discomfort over numbness**, and **responsibility over resignation** - one small decision at a time.

Progress may be slow but it is possible. And with consistent mental investment, compounded over time, the foundation for change begins to take shape.

Level 2: The Survival

Core Belief: "I can get by, but just barely."
Mental ROI: Neutral or minimal - effort produces stability, not progress.
Emotional Landscape: Anxiety, fatigue, cautious hope, fear of slipping backwards.

a. Overview

Level 2 is where many people find themselves after they've escaped a crisis, but have not yet reached stability. They're no longer fully disempowered, but they're still operating in a constant state of financial and emotional tension.

This is the paycheck-to-paycheck reality. Every bill matters. Every setback hurts. There's little room for error - and even less for rest.

People at this level are often working hard, but their effort feels like treading water: **a lot of motion with little forward movement.**

They've made progress - but not enough to feel safe.

b. Common Thought Patterns

- "I just need to make it through this week."
- "If one thing goes wrong, I'm screwed."
- "I want to plan ahead, but I can't afford it."

- "I don't have time to think about long-term goals right now."

At this stage, short-term thinking is a survival mechanism, not a flaw. The nervous system is wired to focus on immediate needs - because for many, missing one payment, losing one shift, or having one unexpected expense can tip the balance into crisis.

c. The Illusion of Progress

Many at Level 2 are extremely hardworking - often juggling multiple jobs, side hustles, or family responsibilities. On paper, they are doing "everything right." But the truth is, they are trapped in reactive mode.

Here's what makes Level 2 so frustrating:

> You're busy, but **not building.**
> You're spending, but **not saving.**
> You're improving, but **still anxious.**

This is the illusion of progress: constant activity that stabilises your current situation but doesn't create meaningful momentum.

d. How Time, Energy, and Attention Are Spent

Resource	Typical Use at Level 2
Time	Spent working, commuting, putting out fires, managing the present

Energy	Consumed by financial worry, decision fatigue, and exhaustion
Attention	Focused on bills, due dates, and short-term planning

The mental investment is narrow and defensive - focused on keeping things from falling apart, rather than building anything new.

e. The Turning Point: From Survival to Strategy

The shift from Level 2 to Level 3 begins when a person can reclaim even a small margin of mental space - to think, plan, and act with intention.

The might look like:

- Automating bill payment to reduce decision fatigue
- Tracking spending for the first time
- Choosing to say no to immediate gratification (e.g. fast food, retail therapy)
- Seeking out free resources (libraries, online learning, community programs)

At this stage, the priority is not big change - it's strategic energy reallocation.

> *Instead of asking, "How can I do more?"*
> *Ask: **"How can I do less, but better?"***

f. Delayed Gratification Strategy at Level 2

The long-term payoff of delayed gratification becomes visible here - but it often feels like a sacrifice without reward. That's why the key is to make it measurable and immediate.

For example:

- If you skip a $10 takeaway meal and cook at home, transfer that $10 into savings immediately.
- If you finish a financial task instead of watching Netflix, reward yourself with an intentional break after.

Delaying gratification only works when the mind can see the **payoff**, even in small ways.

g. Mental Investment Reframe

Default Thought: "I'm too busy to plan ahead."
Growth-Oriented Reframe: "If I create even one system, I free up mental space."

Default Thought: "I'm just surviving."
Growth-Oriented Reframe: "Surviving means I'm still in the game - now it's time to strategise"

-

Level 2 is difficult - not because of failure, but because of pressure.

People here are doing their best with limited resources, and they often go unrecognised. But the key to rising out of this level is not working harder - it's working smarter.

Small systems. Small buffers. Small wins.
Repeated over time.

That's how survival turns into stability.

Level 3: The Worker

Core Belief: "If I work hard and stay consistent, things will improve"
Mental ROI: Linear - input leads to output, but returns are capped by time and energy.
Emotional Landscape: Hopeful, focused, fatigued, often on the edge of burnout.

a. **Overview**

Level 3 represents a shift from survival into **stability**. At this level, basic needs are consistently met, bills are paid on time, and there's enough income to avoid constant stress. People are often employed full-time, freelancing steadily, or operating a dependable side hustle.

This is the realm of the functional middle class where discipline replaces chaos, and structure begins to form. But it's also where many people start to feel stuck in the "work-to-live" cycle.

Effort creates results, but those results are directly tied to how much time and energy they can give. Without them, everything stalls.

b. **Common Thought Patterns.**

- "As long as I keep showing up, I'll be okay."
- "If I just work a bit harder, I'll finally get ahead."
- "I don't have time to think bigger right now."

- "I'm too busy to take the risk - I can't afford to lose this stability."

At this level, hard work is both a strength and a ceiling. The identity of the work can become so ingrained that stepping away from constant doing feels unsafe or irresponsible.

c. The Illusion of Progress

From the outside, Level 3 looks like success. Income is steady. Life is predictable. There may even be signs of upward mobility - a modest savings account, a promotion, a stable routine.

But the danger here is over-identification with productivity.

People at this level may:

- Overwork to feel secure
- Delay rest out of guilt
- Avoid delegation because "no one can do it like I can"
- Choose predictable effort over strategic growth

This creates the illusion that more effort = more progress, when in reality, they've hit a growth ceiling that effort alone can't break.

d. How Time, Energy, and Attention Are Spent

Resource	Typical Use at Level 3
Time	Scheduled tightly - mostly for work, errands, and basic self-care
Energy	Depleted by overcommitment, minimal recovery, and task repetition
Attention	Focused on short-term goals, deadlines, and maintaining routine

The mind is constantly working - not chaotically, like in Level 2, but habitually. And while the structure is comforting, it can become a comfort zone disguised as discipline.

e. The Turning Point: From Worker to Player

The shift out of Level 3 comes from realising this truth:

> *"Effort creates security. But leverage creates freedom."*

To grow beyond this level, one must begin investing in:

- Skills that compound (e.g. leadership, automation, sales, systems thinking)
- Projects that generate income beyond hourly work
- Time for strategic thinking, not just execution

This transition often requires confronting fears around:

- Losing momentum
- Taking calculated risks
- Letting go of control
- Redefining productivity

f. Delayed Gratification Strategy at Level 3

The core struggle here is choosing **long-term leverage** over **short-term completion**.

For example:

- Blocking time to learn a scalable skill instead of clearing more emails
- Turning down a small freelance gig to work on a long-term offer
- Delegating a task - even if imperfectly - to free up creative space

Delayed gratification at this level isn't about spending less. It's about choosing creation over consumption, leverage over labour.

g. Mental Investment Reframe

Default Thought: "If I stop working. I'll lose everything I've built."
Growth-Oriented Reframe: "If I keep doing it all myself, I'll never build beyond this level."

Default Thought: "I don't have time to think big."
Growth-Oriented Reframe: "If I don't make time to think, I'll stay small."

-

Level 3 is where many people plateau - not because they aren't capable of more, but because their systems reward consistency, not creativity.

Comfort is the killer.

Breaking through this level requires courage, not just capacity.
It asks you to stop working harder - and start working wiser.

Your time is limited.
Your energy is finite.
Your focus is precious.

The next level begins when you treat them that way.

Level 4: The Player

Core Belief: “I can make money using my skills - not just my time.”
Mental ROI: Variable - potential for high returns, but dependent on clarity and focus.
Emotional Landscape: Motivated, stretched, inconsistent, energised by possibility, vulnerable to overwhelm.

a. Overview

Level 4 marks a pivotal shift - from structure to strategy. This level is the level where people begin mentising their skills, creativity, or knowledge in a way that is no longer fully dependent on trading hours for income.

Many Level 4 individuals:

- Freelance, consult, or coach
- Run small service-based businesses
- Launch content channels, online products, or digital offers.
- Have income streams with more flexibility than full-time employment

Unlike Level 3, where effort creates predictable returns, Level 4 is about turning skill into opportunity - often through experimentation, iteration, and discomfort.

b. Common Thought Patterns

- “I want to build something that gives me more freedom.”
- “If I don’t try now, I’ll regret it later.”

- "I know I have potential, but I'm not sure how to scale."
- "There's so much I want to do - but I can't focus on one thing."

At this level, ambition is high - but execution may still be inconsistent. Many people bounce between inspiration and imposter syndrome. The vision is growing, but the systems aren't in place yet.

c. The Illusion of Freedom

Level 4 often feels like freedom - because it introduces control over time, location, or pricing. But many people at this level quickly find themselves self-employed but overwhelmed.

The biggest trap here is doing everything yourself:

- Selling, marketing, delivery, admin, design
- Saying yes to every opportunity
- Jumping between ideas, platforms, and business models.

This creates a false sense of growth - lots of activity, low consistency in returns.

The danger? **Burnout dressed as entrepreneurship.**

d. How Time, Energy, and Attention Are Spent

Resource	Typical Use at Level 4
Time	Spent juggling client work, content creation,

	product development, outreach
Energy	Split between building, overthinking, and reacting to opportunities
Attention	Pulled in many directions - ideas, competition, platforms, new tools.

This is the first level where focus becomes the gatekeeper of scale.

e. The Turning Point: From Player to Builder

The transition out of Level 4 begins when you stop being the only asset in your business - and start building assets that work without you.

This might include:

- Productising your services (e.g. digital courses, packages, retainers)
- Creating repeatable systems (e.g. onboarding, delivery, automation)
- Narrowing your offer to one clear niche or transformation
- Reinvesting profits into tools or support

"You're no longer selling time - you're selling outcomes, systems, and strategy."

This level requires deep prioritization. It's not about doing more - **it's about doing less, better.**

f. Delayed Gratification Strategy at Level 4

The challenge here is letting go of immediate wins in favor of strategic depth.

Examples of delayed gratification at this level:

- Turning down short-term projects to focus on building scalable offers
- Investing in software, education, or support before seeing the ROI
- Publishing content without guaranteed engagement to build brand equity
- Taking one offer to mastery instead of launching three new ones.

"Short-term clarity builds long-term consistency."

g. Mental Investment Reframe

Default Thought: "I need to keep saying yes to stay visible."
Growth-Oriented Reframes: "Saying no is how I protect my focus and increase my value."

Default Thought: "I need to do everything myself to save money."
Growth-Oriented Reframes: "Time is my highest cost - not money."

-

Level 4 is exciting, expansive, and full of possibilities

But without clear mental investments, it can become chaotic.

Sustainable success at this level doesn't come from chasing more.
It comes from building better - and trusting that **consistency, clarity and boundaries are the real leverage.**

Your business doesn't scale when you do more.
It scales when you decide what really matters - and build around that.

Level 5: The Builder

Core Belief: "I don't want to just make money - I want to build something that lasts."
Mental ROI: Increasing - effort is being directed toward assets that multiply over time.
Emotional Landscape: Focused, stretched, growth-oriented, navigating control vs. delegation.

a. Overview

Level 5 marks the transformation from being the main operator to becoming a **business builder.**
The business is no longer just a job you created for yourself - it's evolving into a system that can function beyond your direct input. You've moved from playing to building.

Builders start to:

- Hire part-time or full-time team members.
- Create SOPs (Standard Operating Procedures)
- Streamline delivery and automate repetitive tasks
- Standardise their offer and pricing
- Build infrastructure for scale (e.g. backend systems, CRM, processes)

This is where structure and strategic thinking begin to outweigh hustle.

b. Common Thought Patterns

- "I want to step out of the day-to-day, but I don't know how."

- "No one can do it quite like I can - but I can't do it all myself anymore."

- "I finally have money to reinvest - now what?"

- "I don't just want income - I want impact and sustainability."

There's growing awareness that **being busy doesn't equal being effective.**

The goal is no longer just to survive or earn - it's to build something that can run without constant effort.

c. The Illusion of Efficiency

At this level, many founders fall into the trap of over-optimisation:

- They obsess over tech stacks instead of customer needs
- They micromanage because delegation feels risky
- They redesign their branding three times instead of improving conversions.
- They keep refining instead of releasing

This creates the illusion of progress - but it's really **comfort in control** disguised as productivity. True builders learn to **let go** - not because they don't care, but because they understand trust is the engine of scale.

d. How Time, Energy, and Attention Are Spent

Resource	Typical Use at Level 5
Time	Split between strategy, hiring, process refinement, and oversight
Energy	Stretched by the demands of leading others while still executing
Attention	Shifting toward forecasting, metrics, and longer-term decisions

This is the stage where founders realise:

"The bottleneck isn't the business. It's me."

e. The Turning Point: From Builder to Composer

To move toward Level 6, a Builder must shift from being the architect of every system to becoming the **orchestrator of people and outcomes.**

That means:

- Hiring not just helpers - but leaders
- Setting KPIs, not just tasks
- Building a culture, not just a company
- Spending more time on the **vision and strategy** than execution

This transition requires a high level of **emotional intelligence**: letting go of perfectionism, control, and the need to be involved in every decision.

f. **Delayed Gratification Strategy at Level 5**

This level tests your ability to delay recognition in order to build **long-term capacity.**

Examples include:

- Investing in staff training instead of doing it faster yourself
- Spending weeks building systems that save hours later
- Saying no to urgent tasks to focus on important but non-urgent ones
- Withholding the urge to scale revenue until delivery is airtight

"In this phrase, you don't just build income - you build infrastructure."

g. **Mental Investment Reframe**

Default Thought: "It's faster if I just do it myself."
Growth-Oriented Reframe: "If I keep doing it myself, I'll never build something bigger than me."

Default Thought: "My team slows me down."
Growth-Oriented Reframe: "Teaching them now frees me for what matters most later."

-

Level 5 is where vision meets structure.

It’s the difference between being self-employed and being a founder.

Your focus is no longer just on what you can do - but on what you can build.

That means
Less doing, more designing.
Less reacting, more leading.

True builders aren’t addicted to output - they’re committed to outcomes.
And they know that systems, people, and clarity are the ultimate compounding assets.

Level 6: The Team Composer

Core Belief: "My success depends on how well I empower others."
Mental ROI: High - focus and energy are invested into people, systems, and strategy.
Emotional Landscape: Strategic, visionary, emotionally challenged by leadership growth, evolving from operator to conductor.

a. **Overview**

   Level 6 is the point at which your business no longer revolves around you. You've transitioned from builder to conductor - someone who orchestrates people, systems, and processes into something greater than the sum of its parts.

   You've built the foundation. Now, your focus shifts to **team composition, culture building,** and **strategic delegation.**

   Your job is no longer to do everything - it's to **make sure everything gets done through the right people.**

   This is the shift from control to **collaboration.**

b. **Common Thought Patterns**

   - "How do I hire the right people and keep them aligned?"

   - "I want to trust my team more, but I struggle to let go."

- "It's not about me anymore - it's about building something that works without me."

- "Culture eats strategy - how do I shape both?"

This level is less about tactical output and more about leading with clarity, consistency, and **emotional intelligence.**

c. The Illusion of Leadership

Many founders reach this level thinking leadership is about control or charisma. But effective leadership at Level 6 is:

- Quiet when needed
- Clear more than clever
- Consistent, even under pressure

The illusion here is confusing presence with importance. Just because you're not in every meeting or Slack thread doesn't mean you're not leading - it means you've built something resilient.

d. How Time, Energy, and Attention Are Spent

Resource	Typical Use at Level 6
Time	Spent on hiring, 1:1s, strategic planning, team development
Energy	Directed toward building culture, managing

	complexity, and resolving team challenges
Attention	Focused on performance metrics, capacity planning, innovation, and forward-looking goals

This is the level where vision becomes scalable - because others are now helping you carry it forward.

e. The Turning Point From Composer to Sovereign

The next level demands an even deeper shift - from active leadership to **empowered independence.**

To move up, you must:

- Fully trust your leadership team to make decisions
- Step out of day-to-day entirely
- Empower others to lead without your shadow overhead
- Shift your attention to innovation, capacity, partnership, or expansion

This is the difference between running the business - and owning the business.

f. Delayed Gratification Strategy at Level 6

At this stage, your ability to delay gratification is measured by your willingness to invest in people before they're perfect.

Examples include:

- Hiring a promising candidate and mentoring them instead of waiting for the "ideal" hire
- Delegating a key decision even if you could do it faster yourself
- Holding space for team growth instead of micromanaging toward speed

You invest not in tasks - but in **capability.**
And capability compounds.

g. Mental Investment Reframe

Default Thought: "I need to be involved to make sure it's done right."
Growth-Oriented Reframe: "If I'm always involved, I become the ceiling."

Default Thought: "My team needs me for everything."
Growth-Oriented Reframe: "My team grows stronger every time I step back with trust."

-

Level 6 is about **composing harmony**
Not just in operations, but in your culture, communication, and clarity.

You are no longer the executor or even the primary builder, **you are the conductor.**

Your greatest tool is not your hands - it's your **vision, systems,** and **people.**

Leadership here is no longer about being the loudest. It's about making sure everyone else is heard - and aligned toward something meaningful.

When you lead well, the business doesn't revolve around you.

It rises because of you - and grows beyond you.

Level 7: The Sovereign

Core Belief: "My time is best spent owning, not operating."
Mental ROI: Exponential - small decisions have large ripple effects.
Emotional Landscape: Calm, strategic, focused on refinement and preservation; tested by the temptation to reinsert oneself.

a. Overview

At Level 7, you've moved beyond building and leading. You now own a business that can operate, grow, and evolve without your daily involvement.

You are no longer the builder or the conductor - you are the sovereign. You oversee, guide, and govern. But you no longer run the machine. You **own the system** - and the system runs the business.

This is the level where your role becomes one of:

- Long-term strategy
- Brand stewardship
- Capital deployment
- Vision protection
- Cultural integrity

It's not that you do less - you just do far more **high-leverage work.**

b. Common Thought Patterns

- "Where can I create the greatest impact with the least direct involvement?"

- "How do I ensure the vision continues without diluting its essence?"
- "What must I say no to - even if I want to step back in?"

- "How do I balance freedom with stewardship?"

At this level, clarity is your capital.
You lead not with presence, but by principle.

c. The Illusion of Freedom

Level 7 introduces true time freedom - but it also introduces a new challenge: **what to do with that freedom.**

Many Sovereigns fall into one of two traps:
- Re-involving themselves in operations out of habit or ego.
- Drifting aimlessly without a renewed sense of purpose.

Freedom is only fulfilling when paired with **intention.** And intention requires **ongoing clarity** - not just about what the business is doing, but about what you are doing now.

d. How Time, Energy, and Attention Are Spent

Resource	Typical Use at Level 7
Time	Focused on governance, expansion strategy, partnerships, or legacy planning

Energy	Reserved for critical decision, creative visioning, or future-proofing the brand
Attention	Less on operations, more on culture, capital, growth, and legacy impact

This is the level where you manage **attention like a sovereign asset** - because your time is no longer linked to income. It's linked to influence.

e. The Turning Point: From Sovereign to Visionary

To rise to the final level, you must begin shifting from ownership to **inspiration.**
From building businesses… to building belief.

This requires:

- Letting go of needing control, recognition, or relevance
- Prioritising **mission over self**
- Using your story to light the path for others
- Scaling meaning, not just operations

You are no longer building for yourself - you are not **planting shade you may never sit under.**

f. Delayed Gratification Strategy at Level 7

Here, the delayed gratification is **not stepping in** - even when you know you could fix it faster.

It looks like:

- Letting a team member fail safely to help them grow.
- Turning down an exciting project to protect long-term focus
- Choosing not to scale for a quarter to protect culture
- Saying no to “shiny object” opportunities that don’t serve the vision.

“Wisdom is knowing when not to act - even when you can.”

g. Mental Investment Reframe

Default Thought: “I should stay involved to keep things sharp.”
Growth-Oriented Reframe: “If I don’t step back, no one else can step up.”

Default Thought: “I finally have freedom - now what?”
Growth-Oriented Reframe: “Now I ask: How can I serve beyond the business?”

-

Level 7 is not just a financial milestone - it’s a mindset milestone.

You have time.
You have trust.
You have the systems and the people.

Now the question becomes:

What will you do with the space you've earned?

Because this level isn't just about preserving what you've built - it's preparing for something greater.

Not just for yourself. But for others.

You are now a steward of time, vision, and culture.

Lead it well - and you unlock the power to inspire far beyond your walls.

Level 8: The Visionary

Core Belief: "My greatest value is the ideas, movements, and impact I leave behind."
Mental ROI: Infinite - ideas, influence, and intention compound beyond personal involvement.
Emotional Landscape: Aligned, reflective, legacy-driven; occasionally isolated by scale of vision.

a. **Overview**

Level 8 represents the final evolution in the Wealth Dynamics Diamond - where your focus is no longer on income, operations, or business growth, but on **cultural impact, social contribution,** and **shifting paradigms.**

At this level, you are not managing a team - you are leading a **movement.**
You are not building systems - you are shaping beliefs.
Your time is spent in service of something that is **bigger than you,** and you like to outlast you.

This is the space of founders-turned-philosophers, creators-turned-cultural leaders, and entrepreneurs-turned-stewards of global ideas.

b. **Common Thought Patterns**

- "How can I turn this message into a movement?"

- "What legacy am I leaving behind?"

- “How do I use my voice to serve others without becoming the center of attention?”
- “How do I scale meaning - not just business?”

At this level, success is measured not in revenue, but in **resonance** - how deeply your work shifts the lives, mindsets, or future of others.

c. The Illusion of Legacy

Many seek Level 8 recognition - but confuse visibility with **vision.**

Legacy isn’t built by being known. It’s built by being understood - and creating tools, frameworks, or philosophies that people use to change their lives long after you’ve stepped away.

At this level, **humility** becomes the anchor.
You are not the hero.
You are the **mirror** - reflecting back possibility, truth, and transformation.

d. How Time, Energy, and Attention are Spent

Resource	Typical Use at Level 8
Time	Spent sharing ideas, mentoring future leaders, writing, speaking, or advising
Energy	Directed towards causes, cultural contribution, and inner alignment
Attention	Focused on influence, values-based

	leadership, and purpose beyond the self

You are no longer building for scale - your ideas and frameworks are now being **scaled by others**.

e. **From Visionary to Reflection**
   There's no formal "Level 9" but Visionaries often ask:

   "How do I stay grounded while being seen as a symbol?"

   This is the paradox of this level:

   As your impact grows, so does the temptation to lose yourself in the narrative.

   The work now is to ***stay aligned with your truth*** *- even when the world projects something else onto you.*

f. **Delayed Gratification Strategy at Level 8**

   Here, delayed gratification is about trusting the ripple effect.

   - You may never meet the people you inspire.
   - You might not see the fruits of your labor in your lifetime.
   - You write, speak, and teach with no guarantee of outcome - only alignment.

   The reward is **legacy.**
   The ROI is in **generational influence.**

g. **Mental Investment Reframe**

Default Thought: “How do I make a bigger impact?”
Growth-Oriented Reframe: “How can I go deeper in my impact - even if no one sees it?”

Default Thought: “I need to stay relevant.”
Growth-Oriented Reframe: “My ideas are relevant because they’re true - not because I am trending.”

-

Level 8 is not about achievement.
It’s about **alignment.**

You are no longer leading a company - you’re shaping a philosophy.
You are no longer chasing scale - your work now **spreads itself.**

Your presence is not just strategic - it’s symbolic.
You represent what’s possible when someone chooses to build with intention, evolve with integrity, and lead with vision.

You don’t just leave a mark.
You leave a model - one others can follow.

From Levels to Leverage

You’ve now seen the full arc of the Wealth Dynamics Diamond - from survival to sovereignty, from scarcity to significance. Each level demands a different mindset, a new emotional orientation, and a more intentional use of your most valuable resources: time, energy, and attention.

But knowing the map is not the same as moving through it.

> *Healing and change are not peaceful. Change doesn't begin when the pain stops - it begins when you stop running from the pain.*

Progression doesn't come from bypassing discomfort - it comes from staying with it long enough to turn awareness into action.

And you don't have to sprint. You just have to **compound.**

Compound Thinking

The Compound Interest of Thought and Habit

We often hear that wealth is built through compound interest - that small, consistent financial investments grow exponentially over time.

But there's a deeper truth:

> *Your* ***thoughts compound faster than your money ever will.***
> *And your habits are the interest they generate.*

Every thought you repeat - consciously or unconsciously - is a **mental investment** to how successful you will ever be.

You've probably heard the word manifestation - and while it's often dismissed as wishful thinking, neuroscience tells a different story: What you repeatedly focus on literally rewires your brain. It sharpens what you notice, influences what you believe, and determines the action you take - or avoid.

- Scarcity-based thoughts compound into stress, hesitation, and self-sabotage.

- Empowering thoughts compound into confidence, opportunity, and consistent action.

The more a thought is rehearsed, the more it becomes automatic. What begins as a mindset eventually becomes **identity.**

Habits Are the Vehicles of Transformation

If thoughts are the seeds, habits are the growth cycle. What you do repeatedly shapes your trajectory more than what you do occasionally.

This is why the Diamond is dynamic. You don't leap from one level to the next - you **compound into** it.

- Level 1 requires repeated proof that change is possible
- Level 4 requires repeated focus on fewer, better actions
- Level 7 requires repeated restraint - the habit of not interfering

Each level demands a new pattern of thought and a new system of behaviour.

The Real ROI isn't just Financial - It's Mental

- A calm mind in the face of pressure
- A clear plan when others are panicking
- The discipline to focus when distractions abound
- The patience to build when shortcuts tempt you

These are the byproducts of mental and emotional compound interest.

They don't appear overnight. But given enough time and intention, they **multiply in value** far beyond any spreadsheet.

Chapter 3: It Was Never Just a Numbers Game

Why Emotional Safety - Not Spreadsheets - Shapes Your Financial Future

In Chapter 1, we explored how your childhood, past experiences, and core beliefs shape more than just your finances - they shape your worldview. From your sense of self-worth to how you love, trust, avoid, or chase - the foundation of your money story begins long before you ever earned a dollar.

In Chapter 2, we moved from the past to the present. We examined how thoughts are mental investments - how your focus, beliefs, and attention shape your return in life. As your wealth grows, so must your mindset. And with each level of growth comes a new layer of emotional complexity: identity shifts, fear of success, the cost of playing it safe.

> *Despite all the tools - budgeting apps, calculators, spreadsheets, financial literacy courses…*
> *Most people still live paycheck to paycheck.*
> *Most people still overspend.*
> *Most people still avoid checking their bank balance until they absolutely have to.*
> *And most people - even the smart, driven, well-read ones - remain stuck in survival mode.*

This isn't a tech problem.
It's not a knowledge problem.

It's a safety problem.

Most people do not struggle with money because they don't know what to do. They struggle because their body doesn't feel safe enough to do it.

Let that land for a second.

You can download the best budgeting app. Color-code every expense category. Map out your financial goals for the next ten years.

But if your nervous system is dysregulated - stuck in fight, flight, freeze, or fawn - even the most advanced tools will fail.

Because your biology will always override your budget. You were not built to thrive in chaos. You were built to survive it. And for many people, financial stress is not just an inconvenience - it's an emotional trigger. A flash of shame. A punch of panic. A loop of guilt and avoidance that plays on repeat. You already know your money habits are emotional.

So let's zoom out - and look at the world around you. Because if you've ever felt like you're "bad with money," it's not just you. Entire Industries depend on that feeling.

The Business of Dysregulation

How insecurity Became a Billion-Dollar Strategy

The world you live in is not built to regulate you.

It's built to sell to your dysregulation. We live in an economy that doesn't profit when you feel secure. It profits when you feel insecure, not enough, behind.

That feeling of urgency, shame, comparison, or anxiety? It's not a bug. It's a business model.

Healthcare - Wellness vs. Lifestyle

Modern healthcare is one of humanity's greatest achievements. We've extended life expectancy, reduced mortality rates, and developed tools that save lives every day. From vaccinations to emergency surgery, healthcare continues to evolve for the better.

But in a world of fast-paced living and rising health awareness, a new layer has emerged - one that blends **wellness**, **marketing**, and **emotion.**

Today's healthcare system, especially in the consumer space, does more than respond to illness. It responds to insecurity. To the feeling that something might be wrong, even when it's not.

And that's not inherently bad - it's simple reflective of a growing truth:

People want to feel in control of their well-being.
And when we don't feel in control, we often buy reassurance.

Science may save lives. But the system, especially when profit-driven, often profits most when you feel **unwell, uncertain, or not enough**

We are witnessing the rise of a new health frontier - one that blends personal branding, product sales, and wellness culture into an always-on market place. **The Influencer Economy.**

In the age of social media, health has become more than a personal journey - it's a performance. Instagram, TikTok, and YouTube are flooded with morning routine videos that feature shelves of supplement jars, frothy adaptogenics lattes, and affiliate links in the captions.

And here's the issue:
Many of these recommendations are not coming from doctors, nutritionists, or researchers - They're coming from **lifestyle influencers** who've partnered with wellness brands.

Their authority is not based on science. It's based on aesthetics. On having clear skin, good lighting, and the illusion of control. From a marketing perspective brands are not just looking for health experts. They're looking for **reach.** Aesthetic. Authority. A face that sells.

Markets know that most people do not make buying decisions from spreadsheets or PubMed. They buy from emotional resonance. From the people they aspire to be - the person who seems to have it all together.

And so, the strategy is simple:

- Find someone with a clean aesthetic and a loyal following.

- Send them a product.
- Give them a discount code.
- Watch as trust converts into revenue.

These influencers may have no formal training - but they know how to speak to your nervous system:

- They present themselves as aspirational: calm, glowing, disciplined.
- They share their "non-negotiables" - a curated stack of powders, pills, and tinctures.
- They show you the ideal self - not the side effects, not the science, not the long-term implications.

And why should they?

For many, this is not about health. It's about monetisation.

When health becomes a lifestyle brand, the line between wellness and manipulation gets blurry fast.

We don't buy products - We buy perception
Consider this:

> **Panadol** and generic paracetamol have the same ingredient. Same dosage. Same effect. Yet millions still reach for the brand-name box - not because it works better, but because it feels more trustworthy.
>
> People don't say, "I need toothpaste." They say," I need **Colgate**"
> Even though dozens of other brands do the exact same job - often for less money.

Band-Aid vs. adhesive bandages - Band-Aid became the category.
Dettol vs. off-brand antiseptic - The brand “feels” more sterile.
Neutrogenea vs. basic moisturizer - “Dermatologist recommended” builds emotional credibility.

Beauty Profits When you Feel Unworthy.

Insecurity isn’t just a side effect of beauty marketing. It’s the fuel.

From a young age, we’re taught that our appearance is a currency - a measure of value, power, desirability, even success. And in an industry worth over $500 billion, the message is reinforced with surgical precision.

You’re told:

- You need this cream to fight age.
- You need this foundation to fix your skin.
- You need this mascara to lift your confidence.
- You need this serum to stay relevant, attractive, worthy.

The message is never “you are beautiful” but rather,
“You could be beautiful - if you buy this.”

The marketing formula is simple

1. *Create self-doubt*
2. *Offer a cure*
3. *Make it a lifestyle.*

Another disclaimer: There's nothing wrong with enjoying beauty. There's power in self-expression, in rituals, in choosing to present yourself in ways that feel aligned.

The danger is when the choice is no longer yours - but a response to **shame, comparison, or fear of being unseen.**

A 2023 study by McKinsey found that nearly 40% of Gen-Z consumers say they buy beauty products to reduce social anxiety - not to enhance joy.

> *Beauty becomes a performance. And your bank account becomes the cost of staying acceptable.*

And here's a hard truth. **There's no finishing line.**

There's always one more product. One more flaw to target. One more insecurity to monetize.
You're not just spending money - you're spending emotional energy trying to feel "enough".

Education Profits When You Feel Behind

We live in a world where things move fast - new technologies, new careers, shifting industries, changing expectations. So it's no surprise that the education sector has evolved to meet a rising emotional need:

> ***The desire to feel prepared, relevant, and not left behind.***

In fact, many institutions, coaches, and course creators genuinely want to help. But they also understand a deeper psychological truth:

> *People don't always buy education because they want to grow.*
> *Often, they buy it because they're afraid of falling behind.*

And there's nothing wrong with that.

Whether it's a university degree, an online masterclass, or a Udemy course on how to scale your freelance business - education today often serves two purpose:

1. Skill acquisition
2. Emotional regulation

It makes you feel safer. More capable. More in control of your future.

Even if you're not applying the knowledge right away, you're doing something. You're taking action. And that alone offers a sense of relief.

Education as Emotional Insurance

Marketers and course creators understand this. Not because they're manipulative - but because they are paying attention. They know how it feels to scroll through social media and see peers "winning". To hear about someone's six-figure launch. To feel like you missed the wave.

So they speak to that experience - not to exploit, but to motivate action.

> "You're not behind - but you could move faster."
> "The world is changing - let us help you keep up."
> "You have the potential - we'll give you the path."

And honestly, that's not a scam. That's a strategy. That's understanding how people think, feel and make decisions under pressure.

Finance: The Two Faces of Finance

Let's be clear: the finance industry is not the enemy.

There are incredible institutions, advisors, and tools that exist that exist to help people grow their wealth, plan for the future, and build long-term stability.

- Banks offer structured savings plans.
- Superannuation in Australia, 401(k) in the United States. CPF in Singapore provides reliable systems.
- Licensed professionals provide thoughtful, tailored advice.
- Apps now let you track, invest, and budget with unprecedented ease.

These are real solutions - and they work. But, finance is also the most paradoxical industry of all.

> *It promises freedom, stability, and control.*
> *It teaches discipline, planning, and long-term thinking.*

And yet - it often leaves people feeling ashamed, behind, or inadequate.

Not because the system is broken. But because it was built on assumptions that don't always reflect how most people actually behave.

Financial Tools Expect Logic - but Most People Operate From Emotion

Open a budgeting app and what do you see?

- Fancy Piecharts
- Daily spending alerts
- Red warning signs
- Categorised expenses

It's efficient. It's rational. Data-driven.

But for many people, that same screen triggers something deeper:

- Guilt for overspending
- Shame for "not doing better"
- Avoidance, followed by more spending
- A spiral of trying harder... then giving up

Because that's the part the industry rarely accounts for:

Emotion isn't the obstacle to good money management - it's the environment in which all money decisions are made.

And That's Where the Other Face of Finance Steps in.

When long-term structure feels overwhelming, fast relief starts to look attractive.

- Get-rich-quick schemes that promise overnight freedom
- Trading apps with dopamine-triggering charts and real-time competition - even though you're up against millisecond-speed computers and trained institutional traders.
- High-risk crypto projects sold by influencers riding the hype
- Gambling platforms disguised as "investing for fun"

These aren't just "bad decisions." They're **emotionally charged responses** to pressure and pain.

Because when you're not emotionally safe, slow and steady doesn't feel noble. It feels impossible.

You don't crave structure. You crave shortcuts.

Do you see now? Money was Never a Numbers Game

We've spent this chapter unpacking the fact that most people don't struggle with money because they're lazy, unmotivated, or uninformed. They struggle because their nervous system doesn't feel safe.

We spend to feel better.
We spend to feel secure.
We invest to feel hopeful.
We avoid to feel less overwhelmed.
We give to feel connected.
We splurge to feel alive.

Money comes as a medium for emotional transactions - not just a tool for trade, but a reflection of how we regulate uncertainty, signal identity, and construct safety in a complex world.

There's nothing inherently wrong with the way society is shaped.
Marketing exists because storytelling works.
Consumerism thrives because emotion drives decision-making.
Standards form because humans are wired for comparison and belonging.

These are not flaws - they're features of how the world has evolved.

The real problem is not tools - it's fit.

The future of financial design - and consumer wellbeing in general - doesn't live in more dashboards, stricter alerts, or deeper pressure.

It lives in **alignment.**
In tools that respect emotion, that rewards small wins, that nurture identity over shame.

That's the kind of world we should be building.

The Regulation Loop

Why Emotions Repeat Themselves Through Money

Control. Connection. Calm

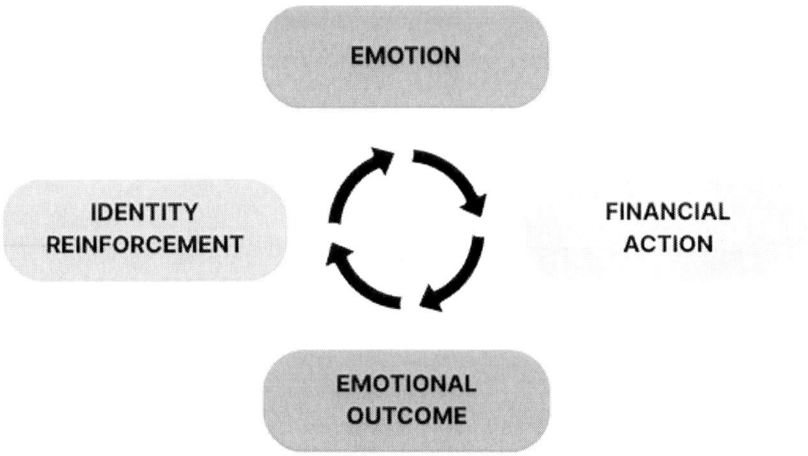

The "Poor" Regulation Loop

You feel stressed after a long day - emotionally depleted, mentally foggy and empty.

That stress needs an outlet. A scroll through your phone showing a flash sale, self-care ad, a friend's travel post.

You click "Buy Now."

And for a moment, it works. You feel better. That's the emotional outcome.

"This is how I soothe."

What's really happening is a regulation loop:
You feel discomfort - stress, boredom, loneliness, anxiety. Your body is searching for relief, You spend, scroll, swipe, or avoid. You feel a temporary sense of control or pleasure. Then guilt arrives. Shame follows. And the cycle repeats.
Eventually, this becomes an identity. You never learned how to pause inside the pattern.

You don't need more discipline. You need **more awareness.**

Let's revisit that same stressful day. Only this time, you pause:

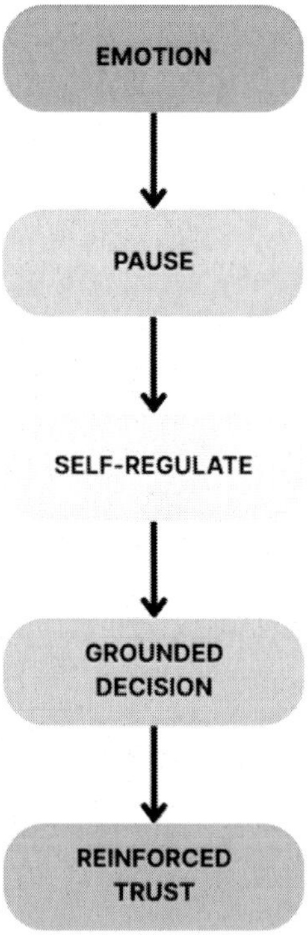

You take a breath. You ask, "What do I actually need right now?"
You journal. You go for a walk. You message a friend.
"Am I making this decision out of fear? Anxiety? Guilt?"

The emotional outcome is different. You feel empowered, not guilty.

Do this enough times, and the loop changes.
Now you're reinforcing a new identity:

"I'm someone who makes intentional choices."
"I can trust myself with money."

When you become more intentional with your money, you become more aware of its flow - not just where it goes, but why. That's the real meaning of **opportunity cost.**

Every dollar you don't spend now isn't just a "saving" - it's a choice. A seed for something more aligned later. The ability to pause, to witness your fear without letting it take the wheel - that's what psychologists call **healthy detachment.**

The Power of Detachment is a Form of Safety.

It creates the space to think, breathe, and choose - instead of reacting.

Detachment give you altitude
Security gives you leverage.
Freedom lets your mind stay expansive - which ironically, attracts more opportunity.

Intentionality isn't about restriction. It's about clarity. It's the shift from autopilot to awareness - from reactive spending to purposeful allocation. Because money is not just a resource. It's a reflection of what you value. Remember money is not just a resource. It's a reflection of your values - and your nervous system. And when you start spending and saving with mindfulness - not fears - your financial life begins to change.

A Gentle Reminder

And still - I know life isn't always this simple. If you're at the earlier levels of the wealth dynamics pyramid - surviving, supporting others, or navigating unstable ground - you might not feel like you even have the privilege of being intentional. Sometimes, life hits hard. I was diagnosed with cancer and was facing a difficult time mentally, emotionally, and financially. I had to seek help from friends and family for help. And it felt like a failure. It felt like weakness.

But looking back now.. there's no shame in that.

This chapter is not about perfection - it's about possibility.
Not about doing more - but seeing differently.

Your self-worth isn't defined by how well you manage money. But by how bravely you keep showing up, even when the system wasn't built for you.

The tools are here when you're ready.
And so is the next version of you.

Chapter 4: The Social Construct of Money - And The Identity it Gave You

Radical Acceptance: Embracing, Unlearning, and Recreating

You Are Not Who You Think You Are

By now, you've probably realised your money habits weren't born in a spreadsheet. They were born in silence, in survival, in moments where you learned what was "normal" - from family, your culture, and your society.

Your values? Inherited.
Your goals? Shaped by others.
Your financial choices? Largely performative - designed to gain approval, avoid judgement, or escape shame.

You learned how to spend long before you learned how to save. You learned what to buy to look successful long before you understood what success actually meant.

> *"I followed society's version of money, until I realised that if I continue living this way, the freedom, the choice, the options I want aren't going to exist. I felt very trapped at that time and I didn't know how to escape."*
>
> - Nischa Shah, Dairy of a CEO

That trap? It's the invisible script - where money becomes a way to perform, not just to live.
Where your identity becomes something you build for the world to see, not something rooted in who you truly are. And if you don't pause to question it, you'll spend your **whole life** trying to be someone who never even felt real to begin with.

> *Most people don't struggle with money because they're lazy or undisciplined.*
> *They struggle because their identity was shaped in a system that taught them who to be, not how to think.*

You were rewarded for fitting in. You were taught to value certainty over curiosity. Stability over authenticity. Status over alignment. So you built a version of yourself the world would accept. A version that knows how to nod, how to hustle, how to hide. But now it's tired. It's starting to ask questions.

This is not just about money. It's about identity. It's about healing the part of you that was shaped by survival. It's time to start rewriting.

Radical Acceptance

Radical acceptance is the practice of seeing yourself - fully, honestly, and compassionately - without trying to immediately fix or judge what you find.

It's saying:

- "Yes, I overspend when I feel unworth - and I understand why."

- "Yes, I've avoided looking at my bank account - and that was my way of protecting myself from pain"
- "Yes, I've undercharged, overworked, played small, performed for approval - and I forgive that version of me."

Radical acceptance doesn't excuse behaviour. It understands it. And in that understanding, something shifts. Not because you force change.. But because shame loses its grip.

Shame is an identity you imposed on yourself. Guilt is a behaviour you can change.

Embracing: A Transactional Mirror

> *"You can't change your future by avoiding your past. You have to sit with it. Not as a punishment, but as a way back to yourself."*

Let's begin here - not in theory, but in practice.
Take a quiet hour. Open your bank account or spending app. Look at your last 90 days of transactions. Not with judgement. Not to fix or feel guilty. But to observe - with honesty and curiosity. You're not just reviewing what you bought. You're meeting the different version of yourself who were present in those moments:

- The one who needed comfort.
- The one who felt lonely.
- The one who wanted to feel in control.
- The one who gave too much.
- The one who didn't believe they deserved more.

It’s about witnessing yourself from a higher lens. So no judgement here.

Step 1: Categorise Your Spending

- Comfort (e.g. food deliveries, retail therapy, alcohol)
- Avoidance (e.g. subscriptions you don’t use, things you bought to “feel better”)
- Validation (e.g. things you bought to impress others of feel “enough”)
- Numbing (e.g. impulse purchases made during stress or boredom)
- Alignment (e.g. purchases that reflect your values, joy, growth, purpose)

Step 2: Meet the Version of You Behind the Spend

Pick 3-5 transactions that carry the most emotional weight - the ones you keep thinking about, regretting, or repeating.

For each one, ask:

- What was I feeling right before I made this purchase?
- What was I trying to soothe, prove, or escape?
- Was I reacting… or responding?
- Did this purchase reflect who I am - or who I was trying to become?

Step 3: Journal with Compassion

Use this following prompts to reflect and embrace that part of you:

1. What version of myself am I still angry at or ashamed of?
   (Describe them in detail. Where were they in life? What did they believe? What were they afraid of?)

2. What was that version trying to feel, or avoid?
   (What emotion were they trying to manage? What need were they trying to meet?)

3. What would happen if I stopped judging that part of me or just listened?
   (What do they need to hear from you now? What does compassion sound like?)

4. Optional: Write a short letter to the past version of yourself.
   "I see you. I know why you did what you did. I know you were trying to feel safe, or seen, or less alone. I don't hate you for it. I love you for surviving the only way you knew how."

Remember

You do not need to erase the past.
You only need to embrace it enough so it stops controlling your future.

Unlearning - Letting Go of the Script That Shaped You

"You don't just wake up one day and become free. You slowly stop believing the stories that were never yours to begin with."

If embracing is about compassionately meeting the version of yourself who coped..
Then unlearning is about challenging what that version believed was true.

It's the part of the journey where you realise:

- You were taught to chase stability, even if it meant abandoning yourself.
- You were rewarded for blending in, not thinking critically.
- You were told that money equals success, and success equals worth.

But just because something feels familiar... doesn't mean it's true.
And just because a belief helped you survive.. Doesn't mean it deserves to lead you anymore.

What is Unlearning?

Unlearning is the process of deconstructing inherited beliefs - about money, identity, value, and success - so you can begin to replace them with truths that align with who you really are.

It's not a **clean break**. It can get **really messy.**

Because most of these beliefs are emotionally charged and deeply embedded in your nervous system. Some of you might stop reading from this point forward, but it's okay. Some of you might not be ready for change. But when the mid-life crisis hits - when career, the car, and the applause stop filling the void - I hope you pick this book up again and remember: It's never too late to return to yourself.

It's the moment you ask:

- Why do I think earning more makes me better?
- Why do I panic when I rest?
- Why do I feel guilty when I spend money on myself?
- Who taught me that success looks like a salary, not satisfaction?

Unlearning requires patience. Because the beliefs you're trying to shed... probably helped you feel safe at some point.

Common Beliefs to Explore

"I'm just bad with money."
"Money doesn't grow on trees."
"Talking about money is rude."
"Debt is shameful."
"I can't be wealthy and a good person."
"Money causes problems."
"If I rest, I'll fall behind."
"I need to work hard to deserve anything."
"I'll always have to struggle."
"Rich people are greedy."

"No one in my family has money, so I probably won't either."
"I'm not smart enough to invest."
"Wanting more makes me ungrateful."
"I need to prove I'm successful."

Now choose your top 2-3. For each one, reflect using these prompts.

1. **Where did this belief come from?**
   (Was it modeled, spoken, or implied? What environment or experience shaped it?)

2. **Is this belief always true?**
   (Can I think of anyone who disproves it? Have I ever disproved it myself)

3. **What does this belief protect me from?**
   (What fear, shame or vulnerability might it be hiding?)

4. **Who benefits from me believing this?**
   (And who suffers?)

5. **What would change if I let this belief go?**
   (How would I act, choose, or feel differently?)

An example:

Unpacking "Money is Dangerous"

When I was younger, my dad misused credit cards. He was in heavy debt. He gambled, borrowed, lost. And eventually, we did too.

There were times when the electricity and water stopped running. I remember the silence before the fights. The stress in the air. The coldness of the room. Money was never neutral at home - it was a loaded gun, passed around recklessly. And every time it went off, it hit all of us.
So I grew up with a nervous system trained to panic around money. It didn't matter how much came in - I couldn't hold onto it. Paychecks disappeared as quickly as they arrived. Spending wasn't sabotage - it was relief. A way to say to myself.

> *"Look, it's gone. You don't have to be scared anymore."*

But I didn't realise then; I wasn't spending money. I was spending anxiety.

Reframed belief:

Money is no longer a threat. It's a tool I'm learning to hold with calm, clarity, and choice. I am not my father. I am the one who breaks the cycle.

Another Example

"Money doesn't grow on trees"

It's a phrase you may have heard from your parents, grandparents, or a teacher when you were young. Maybe you were asking for something - new shoes, a toy, a school trip - and the reply was sharp, quick, and final:

"Money doesn't grow on trees."

On the surface, it sounds practical. Money takes work. It doesn't appear out of nowhere. But the deeper message is subtle - and powerful.

- *Money is scarce*
- *Wanting more is risky*
- *Asking for more is unreasonable.*
- *You should feel guilty for needing or wanting*

For a child, this isn't just a sentence. It's a boundary around possibility. A rule that says: "Stay small. Don't dream too big. Don't expect too much."

Where This Belief Comes From

Many families who lived through poverty, instability, or a lack of opportunity pass this phase down as a warning - a way to teach caution and hard work. It comes from love, but it's rooted in scarcity thinking.

When repeated often enough, it conditions you to believe:

- *Money is hard to get and harder to keep*
- *Only certain people can truly be wealthy*
- *Financial comfort is a rare privilege, not an achievable goal.*

And so, you may work hard… but never truly believe that abundance is possible for you.

Reframed Belief

"Money is a renewable resource. It may not grow on trees - but I can plant seeds, build skills, and create opportunities that allow it to grow in my life."

Recreating - Building From Alignment, Not Fear

"You are not here to simply reject your past. You are here to design your future."

Once you've embraced your past with compassion, and unlearned the beliefs that kept you trapped… You're standing in a rare, powerful space:

A blank page.

Most people never reach this stage because they skip the first two steps. They try to build a new financial life without ever healing the old one. But building without healing is like painting over mold - eventually, the cracks will show.

Recreating is different. It's **deliberate**. It's **value driven**. It's **identity-led**.

The Three Anchors of Recreating.

1. Define "Enough" for Yourself

Most people's financial goals are borrowed - from parents, peers, and influencers.
But chasing someone else's version of "enough" is the fastest way to end up exhausted and unfulfilled.

Ask yourself:

- If no one could see my life, what would I want?
- How much is truly enough for me to feel safe and free?
- Am I chasing numbers.. Or feelings?

Your "enough" becomes your compass. Without it, you're just running in circles.

2. Align Money with Your Values

Money is not just currency - it's a reflection of what you care about.
When you spend in ways that align with your values, every transaction feels lighter.
When you earn in ways that align with your values, every dollar feels cleaner.

Ask yourself:

- What values do I want my money to reflect?
- Where am I spending out of habit, not alignment?
- Do my current money decisions move me toward the life I want?

3. **Create Safety in the Present**

   Your nervous system needs to feel safe before it can hold onto wealth.
   That means creating small, consistent safety cues:

   - An automatic transfer to savings, no matter how small.
   - A few months of expenses in an emergency fund.
   - A no-shame budget that allows for joy and rest.
   - Saying "no" to opportunities that feel off, even if they're profitable.

   The goal isn't just to have money - it's to trust yourself with it.

Here are some reflective prompts for recreating

- What does my financial life look like when it's aligned with my values?
- What daily habits would help me feel financially safe?
- If I stopped trying to prove myself through money, what would I do differently?
- What is my personal definition of "enough"
- What kind of wealth do I want to pass down - financial, emotional, or both?

Recreating your financial identity is not about perfection. It's about ownership. It's about living in a way that says:

> *"I am no longer performing for someone else's life. I am living my own."*

You can't erase the past. But you can decide - starting now - what parts of it are worth carrying forward, and what parts stay behind. And as you step into this chapter, remember:

> ***You are the one who defines enough. You are the one who makes money safe. You are the one who writes the story from her.***

Closing the Loop: From Embracing to Recreating

Radical acceptance isn't a single "aha" moment. It's a cycle you'll return to again and again.

You'll revisit old patterns - not to shame yourself, but to see how far you've come. You'll catch outdated beliefs in the middle of your day - and instead of obeying them, you'll question them. And each time, you'll make a choice:

> Do I return to the old script,
> Or do I write a new line?

You've learned to embrace the version of yourself who coped the only way they knew how - with spending, avoidance, hustle, or playing small. You've met them without judgement and given them the compassion they were starved of.

You've begun to unlearn the stories you never chose - the ones handed down through family, culture, and survival. You've challenged them, on ebay one, until their grip began to loosen.

And now, you're ready to recreate. Not as an act of rebellion against your past, but as a conscious act of authorship for your future.

Recreating is not about "fixing" yourself. It's about choosing yourself. It's about living by your own definition of enough, aligning your money with your values, and creating safety that no one else can take from you.

Remember

You will never feel safe in someone else's story.
You will only feel safe in the one you write yourself.
This is who I am now. This is the life I choose to live.

The Power of Dysfunctional Beginning

The moment we see ourselves clearly - truly, without filters or excuses - is the moment we stop blaming the universe. We stop asking,

"Why me?"

And we begin embracing every jagged, imperfect, extraordinary part of our story.

When we are in tune with who we are - our mind and our worth moving in rhythm with life itself - something shifts. We stop running from the extremes we've felt and start using them.

Those moments of instability, rejection, and dysfunction? They become raw materials. Fuel. Not for revenge or validation, but for purpose.

Wealth, in this frame, is no longer the target. It's the side effect - the natural byproduct of living in alignment with an identity-driven purpose. Some of the m ost impactful leaders in history didn't start life with harmony and security. They started with chaos. They grew up in worlds that were unpredictable, unforgiving, and often unsafe. And they learned to adapt in extraordinary ways.

Case Study 1: Elon Musk

Elon Musk's beginnings were anything but easy. Born in South Africa, he grew up in a household thick with tension and instability. His relationship with his father was fractured from the start - publicly, Musk has described him as emotionally abusive, "a terrible human being" whose influence cast a long shadow over his childhood.

When his parents divorced, Mask made the fateful decision to live with his father. It was a choice he would later say he deeply regretted. Life in that home was far from nurturing. Musk endured not only the turbulence inside his family but also relentless bullying and social isolation at school.

His reguge was elsewhere - in books, in computers, in the limitless landscapes of his imagination. If the world outside felt chaotic and unsafe, the worlds he built in his mind were entirely his own. It was here that the seeds of his identity took root: a dissociation from emotional vulnerability, a preference for mastery and control, a comfort with taking enormous risks.

What began as a shield against chaos evolved into the traits that would define his career: the ability to think on an otherworldly scale, to push beyond conventional limits, and to build entire self-contained realities - whether in video games, electric cars, or the dream of colonising Mars.

Yet the very armour that made him a visionary also carried its shadows: an avoidant attachment style, emotional distance, and the difficulty of letting others close. For Musk, innovation was more than ambition - it was a way of keeping the chaos at bay.

Case Study 2: Bill Gates

Bill Gates grew up in Seattle in an upper middle class home that valued structure, achievement, and ambition. His parents were accomplished and supportive in their own way, but theirs was not an emotionally expressive household. Love was often shown through expectations, not tenderness.

From an early age, Gates stood out as highly intelligent and intensely curious. But he was also restless, resistant to rules that didn't make sense to him. Social norms often felt constraining, and he had little patience for emotional drama.

What he valued - even as a boy - was precision, order, and intellectual challenge.

This inner drive was sharpened by the culture of his home. In a family where performance was the currency of worth, Gates learned that the way to be seen, respected, and value was to excel. His competitive streak became legendary, his focus almost obsessive. Whether it was programming, chess, or academic competitions, he played to win - not just to participate.

This mindset would shape the empire he built. Microsoft wasn't simply a company; it was a manifestation of Gates' need to organise and control systems, to engineer solutions at scale, and to leave an unmistakable mark on the world. His work ethic was unmatched, but so was his tunnel vision.

For years, his emotional world remained secondary to his intellectual one. Even in his marriage, Melinda Gate has spoken about the challenges of bridging that gap - of learning to communicate beyond the language of productivity and results.

Gates' identity was, in many ways still is, rooted in contribution rather than connection. His strength lies in building systems that change the way we work and live. But the same traits that brought him global influence also distanced him from emotional vulnerability. For Gates, mastery was safer than intimacy, and achievement was a language he has learned to speak fluently from the start.

Case Study 3:

Jack Ma's story begins far from privilege. Born in communist China during a period of deep scarcity, his family lived with the weight of poverty and political ostracism. From an early age, he knew what it meant to be on the outside looking in - not just financially, but socially/

School was no refuge. Jack struggled academically and failed China's national university entrance exam twice. Each failure was public and humiliating. He was rejected from dozens of jobs, including one at KFC where, out of 24 applicants, he was one of only two turned away. The sting of rejection became a familiar companion.

And yet, he refused to let those rejections define him. Instead of hardening into bitterness, Jack learned to meet "no" with a smile. He developed an almost stubborn optimism, a belief that setbacks were not personal indictments but simply part of the journey. Where others might have retreated , he leaned into connection - talking to tourists to practice his English, telling stories that drew people in, building bridges with humor and humility.

This approach would become his signature. When he founded Alibaba, it wasn't the story of one man building an empire; it was the story of a group of dreamers working together to transform the way business was done in China. Jack cast a vision big enough for others to see themselves in it, and he led not through fear or dominance, but through a shared sense of possibility.

But even in this light, the shadows remained. Growing up poor and rejected left him with a deep awareness of status and belonging. That internalised shame never fully disappeared - instead, he channeled it into compassion, into making sure others felt seen and included in the vision he was building.

Jack Ma's strength lies not in technological mastery or ruthless efficiency, but in his ability to connect human beings to a cause greater than themselves. His resilience was born from rejection, his leadership forged in humility. For him, success was never about proving people wrong - it was about inviting them along.

The Link?

What links Elon Musk, Bill Gates, and Jack Ma, is not where they were born, how much money they had, or even the industries they chose. It's that each began life in an environment that fractured them.

Musk grew up in Chaos, Gates in emotional distance, Ma in rejection and scarcity.
Each learned, in their own way, that the world was not built to hand them safety or belonging. So they built themselves instead.

Dysfunctional begins force a choice early in life:
You either let instability define you… or you learn to define yourself in spite of it.
In that crucible, identity takes shape - not from comfort, but from necessity. It becomes the compass you carry into adulthood. It decides the way you work, the risks you take, the problems you choose to solve.

For Musk, the answer was mastery and control - crafting entire worlds he could govern when the real one felt ungovernable.

For Gates, it was performance and precision - proving himself through systems that could not be shaken by emotion. For Ma, it was connection and vision - transforming rejection into a mission that made others feel included.

The iron is that what began as a coping became their calling. What once shielded them from pain became the very thing that made them dangerous in the best possible way. Purpose emerged not from ambition alone, but from an unshakable identity forged in adversity. And wealth - vast, generational wealth - followed as a byproduct.

The Contrast: The Quiet Gift of Security

People who grow up secure, rarely know these extremes. Their lives are steady, predictable, balanced. Their sense of self was never under siege, so they never had to build a fortress inside themselves. This stability is a gift - it produces grounded, consistent, emotionally regulated adults. But it rarely forges the same obsessive drive to reinvent, to dominate, to prove.
When you have not lived at the edges of survival, you do not wake each morning with the same raw urgency to reshape the world.

Dysfunction, for all its pain, give you this:
An early and intimate relationship with the extremes of human experience. You've known instability so deep you will do almost anything to never return to it. You've felt rejection so sharp it has carved you into someone unrecognizable from the child you once were. And if you survive it - **really survive it** - you carry a fire that secure people will never fully understand. Like this book I'm writing - half of you readers may not fully understand

it. You may find it too raw, too intense, too far from your own experience.

The lesson from Musk, Gates, and Ma is not to seek dysfunction or glorify suffering.
It's to understand that your beginnings, however fractured, hold raw material for something extraordinary.
You do not have to reject your past to rise above it.
You have to find the parts that taught you resilience, vision, mastery, and turn them into the foundation of your purpose.

When you find yourself. When you stop trying to be the world's version of "enough" and instead align your life with the deepest truths of who you are, purpose becomes inevitable.
And when purpose takes the wheel, wealth becomes almost impossible to avoid.

Chapter 5: The Cost of Comfort

Why Security Can Be the Enemy of Freedom - And How to Build Performance Mentally.

The Comfort of Looking Backward

One of the most seductive forms of comfort isn't a house you can finally afford, a steady paycheck that covers the bills, or even a cushy job with predictable hours. It's the quiet, deceptively safe feeling of endless revisiting the past.

We tell ourselves it's self-awareness. We call it "working on ourselves." In reality, for many people, it's a holding pattern - a way to feel productive while avoiding the risk of moving forward.

Psychology as a discipline has long been split on where to place its gaze: **the past**, or **the future.**

The **past-forcused school** - championed by figures like Sigmund Freud and later Erik Erikson - teaches us that early experiences are the architects of our present. Freud saw the unconscious mind as a vault of childhood impressions and unresolved conflicts, quietly directing our thoughts and actions. Erikson took this further, mapping life into eight distinct stages, each defined by a central conflict. The way we resolved (or failed to resolve) those early conflicts, he argued, would shape every stage that followed.

This perspective has given us language for our pain. It's helped us name patterns, trace their origins, and validate the impact of our beginnings. This is real value here - it can be the starting point of deep healing.

But it has also created a subtle trap: the belief that to move forward, you must endlessly examine what came before. And that's where comfort sneaks in. Society has a deep appetite for looking backward, and it's not just a matter of curiosity. It's cultural, emotional, and **commercial.**

> *If you can understand what happened to you, you can fix what's happening to you.*

And to a point, that's true. Understanding can be liberating. Naming your pain can be the first step in releasing it. But the industry built around this understanding has every reason to keep you looking backward - because it's profitable.

Weekly therapy sessions. Self-discovery retreats. Endless courses, workshops, and online programs about "finding your true self" through your past. The market for therapeutic and wellness services is worth $6.3 trillion dollars as of 2025, and much of it is structured around the idea that there's always another layer to unpack, another wound to process.

Therapists who work primarily in this space aren't necessarily trying to trap you - most genuinely want to help. But the structure of past-focused therapy rewards continuity over closure. The more you believe you have to keep digging to heal, the longer you stay in the chair.

And society reinforces it. We glorify the act of "working on yourself" when it looks like reflection. We celebrate vulnerability when it's about telling old stories. We rarely applaud someone for simply moving forward, for quietly rebuilding without turning it into a narrative.

Future-focused growth - taking decisive action, embracing discomfort, building something new - is far less marketable. It doesn't feed into the endless content cycle of sharing your wounds. It doesn't keep you subscribed to a process that costs $200 an hour. And it doesn't sell nearly as well as a workshop on "unlocking your past to heal your present."

So we stay in the loop:

> *Talking about our past.*
> *Revisiting our past.*
> *Analysing our past.*
> *Because it feels important. Because it feels safe.*
> *And because it's been sold to us as the path to transformation - even when transformation actually lives in the uncertainty of the future.*

Why Stability Feels Safe but Quietly Erodes Growth

Your nervous system is wired to crave safety. After years in survival mode, stability feels like relief - the deep exhale after holding your breath for far too long. But here's the thing: your brain doesn't want to feel safe - it wants to stay safe.

That's the problem.

The same stability that protects you also convinces you to stop reaching. You stop chasing hard goals because you don't need them anymore. You avoid risks because you've now got something to lose. You start guarding what you have instead of building what could be.

In chapter 2 where we talked about the Wealth Dynamic Pyramid, most people get stuck at the worker level. Why? Because comfort tricks you into thinking you've arrived.

You buy the house. You spend your whole life paying off the debt. You take the annual vacation. You finally feel stable - and the relief is intoxicating. You declare to yourself, **"I've made it."**

And to escape the bottom. That is worth celebrating. But this is exactly why it's important to understand what enough means to you.

Trade offs:

> *If you want a family, you might have to sacrifice certain freedoms.*
> *If you want to travel extensively, you might have to delay starting a family.*
> *If you want to build serious wealth, you might have to pass on short-term comforts.*

Without clarity on what enough means, you'll either chase endlessly or stop far too soon. Comfort will make the choice for you - and it will almost always choose **"stop."**

Comfort vs Freedom

Most people mistake comfort for freedom. They're not the same thing.

Comfort *- is the absence of discomfort.*
Freedom *- is the ability to choose discomfort on your own terms.*

Comfort is fragile. *Lose your job, watch the economy turn, face a sudden illness - and your entire sense of security shatters.*
Freedom is durable. *It's built on adaptability, skills, assets, and resilience that hold steady even when the world tilts.*

Comfort *says: "Protect what you have"*
Freedom *says: "Build so much you can't lose"*

Comfort *makes you guard the present.*
Freedom *makes you design the future.*

If you value comfort more than freedom, you will quietly trade away growth for the illusion of safety.

The Turn Tables

By now, you've looked the past in the eye. You've traced the patterns, named the mistakes, and seen where you've been holding yourself back.

That's enough.

Reflection is a powerful teacher, but it's a terrible home. You cannot build your future in the ruins of your past. At some point, you must decide:

This version of me is finished and no longer serves me.

I want you to read your past reflections one last time. See them clearly. See the wins, the failures, the heartbreak, the lessons - all of it. And then I want you to **rewrite it everyday.**

Where you once saw rejection, write resilience.
Where you once saw weakness, find wisdom.
Where you once saw shame, make space for self-compassion.

This is not about pretending the past did not happen. It's about refusing to let it define what happens next. From this point forward, you are not carrying the weight - you're carrying the lesson. You have to stop repeating the pattern by rewriting your identity. Life will test you and old patterns will suffice but that's okay. We just need to put more consciousness into our unconsciousness. Telling ourselves we deserve **better.**

(Journal prompts to guide your daily rewrites are at the end of this chapter.)

High-Performance Psychology: Building the Mental Framework for Sustained Success

"If I'm not defined by my past anymore.. How do I build my future?"

The answer? **High-Performance Psychology** - The science and practice of optimising your mind for sustained success under pressure - whether that pressure comes from competition, leadership, entrepreneurship, or everyday demands of building a life worth living.

High-performance psychology is about deliberately creating the mental, emotional, and environmental conditions that make growth your default state.

It's proactive, not reactive.
It's forward-focused, not backwards-looking.

What is High-Performance Psychology?

High-performance psychology is the mental performance training system used by elite athletes, military units, top entrepreneurs, and high-stakes leaders.

It blends:

- **Evidence-based frameworks**
  grounded in behavioural science, leadership research, and sport psychology.

- **Immersive, pressure-based practice**
  training the mind under simulated challenges so it's ready when the stakes are real.

- **Reflective processes**

reviewing performance to improve decision-making and mental resilience.

- **Measure and accountability**
  tracking progress with metrics that matter.

It's not about hoping you'll perform well when it counts. It's about engineering the conditions so you always perform well when it matters.

Lessons from High-Performance Sport and Why This Matters Beyond Sport

In elite sport, mental performance is as important as physical conditioning. An athlete can be the most technically skilled in the world, but without the ability to focus, adapt, and recover mentally, their career will crumble under pressure.

One leader in this space is Dr. Rosanna Stranimirovic, PhD, whose research and applied work with the Australian Institute of Sport focuses on embedding mental performance directly into the daily fabric of training. Her work isn't about last-minute pep talks or quick-fix motivation - it's about turning mental excellence into part of the team's DNA.

Dr. Stanimirovic's approach transforms mental skills from a "nice-to-have" into a **non-negotiable performance pillar.** It's built on the foundation of **Self-Determination Theory**, which shows that sustained motivation comes when three psychological needs are met: **Autonomy, Competence, and Relatedness.**

When athletes feel **ownership over their training** (autonomy), believe they **can improve** (competence), and know they're **supported** (relatedness), they stop performing just to please others - and start performing because they want to.

a. Need-Support Coaching Behaviours

Leadership that builds resilience and self-determination rather than dependence.

Example:
In the lead-up to the 2020 Tokyo Olympics, Australian diver Melissa Wu was battling injuries. Instead of forcing her to push through the same punishing routines, her coach adapted training to include visualisation, technical breakdowns, and strategic rest. This gave Wu a sense of control over her recovery and rebuilt her confidence - without losing competitive edge. She went on to win bronze.

Takeaway:
By meeting her need for autonomy and competence, Wu stayed motivated and mentally engaged. In any field - sport, business, or life - when leaders empower people instead of

controlling them, performance becomes self-sustaining.

Why this matters beyond sport:

- In wealth:
  You stick to an investment plan far more consistently when you've designed it yourself instead of blindly following someone else's tips.

- In leadership:
  A team member who owns their project will take more initiative than one who's micromanaged.

- In relationships:
  Giving your partner space to grow builds trust and mutual respect, instead of dependency.

Need-supportive leadership transforms people from simply following orders to actively owning their performance.

b. Integrated Mental Skills Training

Mental tools for focus, composure, and adaptability practised daily - not saved for game day.

Example:

Richmond Football Club in the AFL integrates short mindfulness and reset drills before every training session - not just before matches. This conditions players to regulate their focus instantly, even mid-play. In the 2019 AFL Grand Final, after a shaky first quarter, senior players used these reset cues to steady the team and shift momentum, leading to a dominant win.

Takeaway:
Mental skills are like muscles - they only grow through repetition. You don't wait until a crisis to train them. By embedded mental resets into daily practice, athletes make composure and clarity their default state.

Why this matters beyond sport:

- In wealth
  Reviewing your money and investment strategy weekly builds the reflex to stay calm during market dips.

- In leadership
  Regularly practising constructive feedback makes difficult conversations less intimidating.

- In relationships
  Daily gratitude or communication habits prepare you to handle conflict without panic.

When you make mental skills part of your everyday life, high performance stops being a switch to flip - it becomes who you are.

c. Whole-Team Adoption

Everyone speaks the same mental language - coaches, players, and support staff.

Example:
In elite cycling, Team Jumbo-Visma uses a unified resilience strategy. When a rider crashes, every staff member - from coach to mechanic - reinforces the same message: focus on recovery and progress. This approach helped Primoz Roglic mentally rebound from a brutal 2021 Tour de France crash and return to win the 2022 Vuelta a Espana.

Takeaway:
Mixed messages create confusion. A unified mental framework ensures everyone is pulling in the same direction, which amplifies resilience and focus.

Why this matters beyond sport:

- In wealth
  Aligning your family or business partners on shared financial values prevents sabotage and second guessing.

- In leadership
  A team that shares the same language for goals and priorities moves faster and with less conflict.

- In relationships
  Shared values act as the compass for making decisions together.

When everyone operates from the same mental playbook, momentum compounds - in sport, in business, and in life.

d. Performance Tracking

Mental readiness is measured as seriously as physical stats.

Example:
The Australian women's hockey team tracks heart-rate variability (HRV) and mental readiness daily. Before the Commonwealth Games, coaches spotted a player whose mental fatigue spiked after consecutive high-intensity days. Adjusting her recovery plan boosted her match-day consistency - she became a key contributor in Australia's gold-medal win.

Takeaway:
What gets measured get improved. Tracking mental readiness makes performance tangible and actionable instead of leaving it to chance.

Why this matters beyond sport:

- In wealth
  Tracking your spending, savings rate, and net worth ensures you spot problems early and adjust before damage is done.

- In leadership
  Tracking employee engagement helps you identify burnout before it becomes resignation.

- In relationships
  Regularly checking in on emotional connection prevents small rifts from becoming long-term distance.

When you measure your mental performance as seriously as your results, you stop guessing and start growing.

The four pillars you've just read about are not just for Olympians or professional athletes - they are universal. They work in the pool, on the field, in the boardroom, in your **bank account,** and even your kitchen table. How you do one thing, is how you do everything. Knowing these theories is not enough. The gap between understanding and transformation is application. High-performance is not something you remember when it's convenient; it's something you build into the fabric of your daily life so it becomes who you are.

That's where your high-performance framework comes in. It's the bridge between the theory and the life you want - a personalized system that takes the principles of elite sport and hardwires them into your own routines, decisions, and environments.

Designing your Personalised High Performance Framework

> *The **BEST** self help book is a parenting book. You need to learn to be the parent of your inner-child. The truth is nobody is going to be there for you but yourself.*

1. Lead Yourself Like a Supportive Coach

Don't wait for someone else to set your standard - set it yourself.

If you live by someone else's expectations, you'll spend your life chasing their approval instead of building a life that's meaningful to you. The world is full of ready-made templates for how you should live - how much you should earn, what kind of work you should do, even how you should spend your free time. But those templates aren't written by you. They're designed to keep you in line with the crowd.

The challenge is, most of us don't even realise we're following someone else's script. You don't know what you don't know. If you've been shown a different way, it's easy to believe the way you're living now is the only option. That's why learning - actively seeking out new knowledge - is critical. The right ideas can crack open your perspective and show you possibilities you didn't even know existed.

One of the fastest ways to expand your awareness is by reading books and listening to people who have walked the path you want to walk. If you want to master your finance Nischa Shah's work on personal finance can save you years of trial and error. If you want to understand high-level thinking and the mindset of world-class entrepreneurs, Steven Bartlett's Diary of a CEO podcast is a deep dive into decision-making, resilience, and problem-solving. And there are countless others - Atomic Habits for building systems that stick, Principles by Ray Dalio for navigating complex decisions, Shoe Dog by Phil Knight for the raw truth about building something from nothing.

But here's the key: Don't just absorb their ideas - adapt them. Take what resonates, discard what doesn't, and shape your own approach. Because the point isn't to live exactly as they have; it's to equip yourself with the mental tools, strategies, and lessons that will allow you to set your own standard.

2. Practice Metal Skills Daily

Don't wait until under pressure to work on your mind. By the time the high-stakes moment arrives, it's too late to start building the mental resilience you'll need. Just as an athlete trains their body before stepping onto the field, you need to train your mind before life demands it.

The problem is that most people only think about mental performance when things go wrong. They lose their temple in a meeting, panic when the market drops, or freeze during a difficult conversation - and only then do they say, “I really need to work on that.” But that’s like deciding to start running sprints halfway through a race.

The secret is to practice when the stakes are low, so when the pressure rises, the skill is already wired into you. Review your finances regularly, not just when you’re worried about them, so you can make calm, confident adjustments when the market turns. Practice delivering constructive feedback in everyday conversations, so that when the high-pressure meeting comes, your words are measured and effective. Build communication habits in your relationships during peaceful times, so that when conflict inevitably arises, respect and clarity guide the conversation instead of anger.

Choose one mental skill you want to strengthen - focus, composure, or adaptability - and commit to working on it for just five minutes a day. Visualise staying calm under pressure. Practice pausing before you react. Train yourself to reframe problems as challenges instead of threats.

Do it often enough, and you won’t have to “try” when life tests you. You’ll simply respond like someone who’s already prepared - because you will be.

3. Align Your Environment

Your surroundings should make performance easier, not harder. If you're constantly swimming against the current of the people, systems, and habits in your life, no amount of willpower will keep you from burning out.

The truth is, some environments quietly sabotage you. A friend who constantly dismisses your goals. A work culture that rewards busyness over results. A cluttered system that makes every decision harder than it need to be. These are not neutral forces - they pull you off course, sometimes without you even noticing.

Ideally, you'd be surrounded by people who push you forward, hold you accountable, and celebrate your wins. But the reality is, you might not be that lucky - at least, not yet. Many people discover that when they start aiming higher, they begin to outgrow their old circles. Friends, colleagues, even family might not understand your ambitions. That can feel lonely.
But here's the thing: you can still choose who influences you. Books and podcasts are another form of "surrounding" yourself with the right people. Reading a book is like having a private conversation with the author - sitting down for an hour with their best insights, their mistakes, and their strategies for success. The more you read, the more mentors you'll have. The more you listen to podcasts from people who have already climbed the mountain, the more you'll realise that your

challenges are not unique - and that the climb to the top is often a solitary path.

If you want your environment to work for you, start by taking inventory. Who in your life lifts you up? Who drains your energy? Which habits push you forward, and which ones hold you back? Identify one person, habit, or system that undermines your goals and either replace it or redesign it to support you.

Your environment isn't just where you live - it's everything you allow to shape your thinking. When you choose that intentionally, success stops being an uphill battle and starts feeling like a natural direction.

4. Measure What Matters

If you can't measure, you can't improve it. But here's the mistake most people make: they try to measure everything and end up tracking nothing that truly matters.

You don't need endless spreadsheets or fancy tools. You just need to keep your focus on the four foundational areas that shape the quality of your life. I call them the Four Daily Wins. They're not arbitrary. They're the core building blocks of personal growth, resilience, and freedom. Get these right, and every area of your life gets easier.

Number 1: Physical Win - Your Energy is Your Engine

Your body is the container for every goal, decision, and relationship you'll ever have. When you train your body - whether it's running, lifting weights, stretching, or training - you're not just building muscle or burning calories. You're training discipline, fortifying resilience, and sharpening mental clarity. A strong body supports a sharp mind. And when your physical energy is high, you can approach every challenge with greater intensity and focus.

Number 2: Mental Win - Your Mind is Your Compass
Your decisions will only ever be as good as the quality of your thinking. Reading, reflecting, and learning something new expands the mental maps you navigate life with. Most people feed their mind with endless distraction - scrolling, snacking on soundbites, consuming without thinking. But depth is what changes you. Books, long-form podcasts, and real reflection give your mind the raw materials to solve bigger problems and make better decisions. A sharper mind means fewer wasted years.

Number 3: Financial Win - Your Freedom Depends on it
Money isn't everything, but without financial agency, the choices are limited. When you build something, work deeply, save, or invest, you're buying yourself more than possessions - you're buying time, options, and independence. Financial wins compound over time, and the earlier you start stacking them, the sooner you can live life on your terms instead of renting your time to someone else's dream.

Number 4: Spiritual Win - Your Anchor in the Chaos
In a noisy, hyper-connected world, stillness is a competitive advantage. Whether you pray, meditate, journal, or practice gratitude, these moments reconnect you to what matters most. This isn't about religion - it's about alignment. Stillness breeds clarity, and clarity keeps you grounded when life shakes you. Without it, you drift into living reactively, constantly pulled by other people's demands of your own priorities and you call this **"fate".**

Start simple. Commit to these four wins each day. They are the foundation. As time passes, you'll naturally dive deeper into each one - refining your training, sharpening your thinking, strengthening your financial strategy, and deepening your spiritual clarity.

It's a simple equation:
Win more days, you win the week.
Win more weeks, you win the month.
Win more months, you win the year.
Win more years, you win LIFE.

5. Review, Adjust, Repeat

High performance isn't "set and forget". It's a cycle. You don't build a winning life by making one perfect plan and sticking to it blindly. You build it by constantly reviewing, refining, and adapting as you go.

The world changes. Your circumstances change. Your priorities change. The strategy that worked last year might hold you back this year. The routine that kept you sharp six months ago might now feel stale. If you don't take time to step back and review, you risk drifting off course without even noticing.

The best performers in every field understand this. They pause to ask the hard questions:

> ***What's working? What's slipping? What's no longer serving me?***

This is where the **Four Daily Wins** become your compass. Your first physical win might be something small - like running 5km. Once you've mastered that, maybe it's 10km. Then a half marathon. The point isn't distance - it's that you're pushing the edge of what's comfortable, step by step.

A mental win might start as simply as reading 5 pages of non-fiction books a day. At first, that might feel ambitious. But once it becomes a habit, you'll start seeking out more challenging material, diving deeper into topics, and applying what you learn in new ways.

Financial wins can be equally simple in the beginning - maybe saving $50 a month. It's not about the amount; it's about proving to yourself you can set aside money constantly. That small win creates momentum, and momentum makes bigger wins possible.

Your spiritual win might be as straightforward as looking in the mirror every morning and saying five things you are grateful for. It might feel awkward at first. But keep doing it, and you'll be training your mind to look for the good in your life before it searches for the bad.

Schedule a monthly review. Look at your progress in each of these areas. Celebrate the wins. Adjust the goals. Push a little further where you can. Pull back and reset if something's not working.

Because high performance is not about perfection. It's about deliberate, ongoing evolution. You don't just set the course once. You keep steering.

Have you ever thought to yourself, "I wish I knew then what I know now" or "If only I'd started earlier"?

Today is the youngest you will ever be. You will never again have this exact combination of time, energy, and opportunity. Every day you wait, the starting line moves further away.

Most people think waiting costs them nothing. They think they'll start when the timing feels better, when the pressure is lighter, when they're "ready". But delay isn't neutral - it's **debt.** The longer you wait to take ownership of your growth, the more compounding returns you lose. Just like investing, the earlier you start, the greater your return over time.

You don't need to have everything figured out to begin. You just need to start stacking wins, one day at a time. And to do that, you have to understand something most people get wrong: it's not about time management - it's energy management. You can have the perfectly organised calendar, but if you show up to it drained, distracted, and depleted, it won't matter. Energy is the currency of performance. The Four Wins you've been learning aren't just habits - they're daily deposits into your energy account. Each one fuels the others.

When you live this way long enough, something shifts. You stop thinking of high performance as something you do occasionally, when the stakes are high or motivation strikes. It becomes who you are. You're no longer a person who "tries" to be disciplined - you are disciplined. You're no longer chasing success - you're living it. And that identity shift is the most powerful force you can harness, because behaviour follows identity. Once you see yourself as the kind of person who wins the day, reviews the week, and pushes a little further each month, you will fight to keep that identity alive.

One day, you'll look back and realise that you've become the person you once hoped you'd be - not because you waited for the perfect moment, but because you stopped waiting altogether.

Journal Prompts (The Gym for Your Mind)

Step 1: Name it

- What happened today or in the past that still lingers in the mind?
- What emotions does it bring up?

Step 2: Reframe it

- What's the lesson or strength hidden in this?

- How could this have been preparing me instead of punishing me?

Step 3: Rewrite it

- Write a one-sentence new identity statement as if it has always been true.
- Keep it positive, present-tense, and powerful.

Step 4: Anchor it

- What action can I take today to live in alignment with this new identity?

Examples:

At work:

Today my manager told me I was too slow in delivering the report and did not hit all my KPIs. I feel frustrated, a bit defensive, and worried they see me as underperforming.

This feedback shows me exactly where my blind spots are and does not define who I am. It is not personal but rather giving a map to improve.

I am the kind of person who takes feedback as fuel, not fire. Every critique makes me faster, clearer, and more precise. I'll follow up regularly with my manager, and ensure I keep myself on pace, and send a draft earlier for quick feedback.

Someone cuts you off in traffic:

Someone just swerved in front of me without indicating. My first reaction was anger: "People are rude and selfish".
This is a moment to practice patience. I can't control other drivers, but I can control my own state. My safety and peace matter more than proving my point. I am the kind of person who stays calm and protects my peace, even when others are reckless. I'll take a deep breath, loosen my grip on the wheel, and put on a song and enjoy to reset my mood.

A friend cancels plans last minute

My friend just cancelled dinner an hour before we were meant to meet. I feel my time is not respected. This frees up space I did not expect to have. I can use it for something that moves me forward - resting, reading, or working on my own goals. I am the kind of person who values my time and uses it well, regardless of other people's schedules. I'll make a cup of tea, open the book I've been meaning to finish, and enjoy this unexpected pocket of time.

These are negative triggers but it is important to focus on the positive triggers in life too.

A stranger compliments my work
Someone told me my project was impressive. It felt good, but I almost brushed it off. This shows my effort is being seen and valued. I should own that without downplaying it. I am the kind of person whose work inspires and adds value to others. I will write down the compliments in my wins journal to revisit on tough days.

I completed a workout i did not feel like doing
I pushed through the workout even though I wanted to skip it today. This proves I follow through on commitments to myself. I am the kind of person who shows up even when it's inconvenient. I will schedule my next workout while momentum is fresh.

I helped someone without expecting anything back
I gave my time to a colleague who was struggling.This is how I build trust and social wealth over time. I am the kind of person who invests in others' success without keeping score. I will send them a quick message later to check in on how they are doing.

Chapter 6: Social Wealth & Network Capital

Wealth is Barely Built Alone

We love the myth of a self-made person. The lone wolf. The visionary who fought against all odds and built an empire with nothing but grit and late nights. It's inspiring, romantic, and often a lie.

Rarely does one succeed alone. Behind every "self-made" success story is an invisible web of mentors, collaborators, allies, and gatekeepers. Someone opened the first door. Someone vouched for them in the room they weren't in. Someone took a risk on them when they had no track record.

Even the people we idolise for their independence didn't climb alone. Steve Jobs and Steve Wozniak. Elon Musk had the PayPal Mafia. Oprah had mentors and producers who believed in her before the audience did.

Your network is not just a list of contacts. It's your social infrastructure - the people who give you access to opportunities, resources, and information you could never get alone. The stronger your network, the more leverage you have. The weaker it is, the harder and slower your climb becomes.

But here's the catch: most people treat their network like an afterthought. They focus on building skills, chasing money, and hitting personal goals, assuming the relationships will "just happen" along the way. They don't. And when the moment comes that you need someone to vouch for you, open a door for you, or pull you up a level, you'll discover that network capital - just like financial capital - only exist if you've been building it all along.

Social wealth is the compound interest of relationships. Every conversation, every introduction, every moment of genuine value you create for someone else is a deposit. And like money in an investment account, those deposits grow quietly in the background until, one day, they open doors you didn't even know existed.

The question isn't whether you need a network. You already have one. The real question is whether you're managing it like a random contact list or as your most valuable asset.

What Social Wealth Really Is

Social wealth is not about collecting people. It's about collecting trust.

It's the accumulation of goodwill, credibility, and mutual respect you've built over time. It's the unspoken equity you hold with the people in your life - the sense that if you called, they'd answer, not out of obligation, but because they know you've given them value before.

The easiest way to think about it is as a **compound interest for relationships**. Every time you help someone without expecting anything in return, you're making a deposit. Every time you show up consistently, following through on a promise, or connect two people who can help each other, you're adding to your balance. Over time, those deposits grow into something far more valuable than any single transaction: **reputation capital.**

And here's the paradox - the people with the most social wealth rarely have to "network" in the traditional sense. Opportunities, collaborations, and introductions start flowing to them without asking. Why? Because they've built such a high level of trust and goodwill that their network works on their behalf, even when they're not in the room.

Social wealth is also multidimensional.

- **Information Capital**
  Access to insights and knowledge that others don't have.

- **Opportunity Capital**
  Invitations, introductions, and deals you wouldn't have found alone.

- **Influence Capital**
  The ability to move ideals, inspire action, and create momentum through your relationships.

It's not about having the most contacts on your phone. It's about having the right people in your corner - people who are invested in your success because you've been invested in theirs.

The truth is, most people never consciously build this. They stumble into relationships, treat them transactional, or neglect them until they need something. That's like ignoring your bank account until you want to buy a house.

Social wealth is built before you need it. Its an insurance policy against obscurity, stagnation, and isolation. And the earlier you start building it with intention, the more powerful it becomes over time.

The Three Layers of Networking Capital

Your network isn't one big, homogeneous blob of "people you know." It's layered - and each layer plays a different role in your life. Understanding these layers is crucial, because it helps you focus your energy where it matters most while still keeping the outer edges alive.

1. The Inner Circle - High Trust, High Leverage

This is your core. The people who will pick up your call at 3 a.m. The ones who know your ambitions, your blind spot, and your values. They're invested in your success at a personal level, not just a professional one.

You don't need many people in this circle. The smaller the better. Quality beats quantity. These are the mentors who guide you, the partners who build with you, the friends who'll fight for you in rooms you're not in. They're your advocates, advisors, and allies all rolled into one.

Your Inner Circle is where trust runs deepest and leverage is highest. Protect these relationships fiercely. Nurture them regularly. If this circle weakens, everything else in your network suffers.

2. The Middle Circle - Active Collaborators

These are your professional peers, industry contacts, and collaborators. You know each other well enough to work together, share resources, and recommend each other, but you're not deeply entwined in each other's personal lives.

The Middle Circle is where most opportunities happen. This is where you meet co-founders, referral partners, suppliers, and collaborators. The key here is reciprocity - being known as someone who follows through, adds values, and makes good introductions.

You may not speak to these people every week, but you check in often enough to keep the relationship warm. That warmth is critical. Cold networks rarely produce hot opportunities.

3. The Outer Circle - Weak Ties, Strong Potential

Your Outer Circle is made up of acquaintances, casual connections, and people you might only interact with a few times a year. At first glance, this layer can feel unimportant - but research consistently shows that weak ties create the biggest leap forward.

Why? Because they exist outside your immediate circle and bring in information, opportunities, and perspectives you wouldn't otherwise see. A friend of a friend might introduce you to your next investor. A casual Linkedin connection could connect you to a dream client.

The trap here is neglect. Outer Circle relationships fade quickly if you never touch base. Even a brief comment on a social post, a congratulatory message, or a quick coffee can keep the connection alive long enough for the right moment to strike.

Manipulation vs. Persuasion - The Ethics of Influence

Confidence. Acceptance. Groundedness.

These are not hacks. They are not surface-level affirmations. And they cannot be faked - not forever.

You've probably heard "Fake it till you make it."
It works... until it does not. Yes, sometimes confidence is a muscle you build by acting "as if" - but long-term authenticity can't be forged through performance. Frank Abganale, immortalised in Catch Me If You Can, pulled it off for years - impersonating professionals, forging his way through life with nothing but borrowed confidence and a sharp mind. But beneath the charm was emptiness. His success was reaction, not foundation. The outer world admired him, but the inner world never felt safe.

That's why this book did not start with what to do. It started with who you are. The parts you avoid. The wounds you carry. The beliefs you inherited. The shadows you never gave a name.

Because without that work, no strategy will stick. Not financially. Not relational. Not professional.

And here's the most humbling realisation of all:

> *The more self-aware you become, the more blind spots you uncover.*

The more emotionally intelligent you grow, the more nuanced life becomes. You begin to see how complex people are. How fragile success is. How little we control. You stop needing to win every argument, impress every room, or chase every goal - because you finally realise that depth matters more than dominance. This is what true wisdom looks like. Not louder. Not faster. Not shiner. Just **quieter confidence**, built through lived experience and open curiosity.

You start reading more, not because you're lost but because you finally awake to how much there is to learn. You start listening more - to mentors, to podcasts, to people who've been where you want to go. Not to copy them, but to understand the deeper principles they live by.

The Gravity of Real Confidence

When you stop trying to impress people, you begin to attract them. It's a paradox: the more you chase approval, the more it eludes you. But the moment you stop performing, you become magnetic. Not because you are louder, more talented, or better looking, but because you radiate something most people don't even know they're craving.

> *Stability. Clarity. Presence.*

Confidence is not about being better, it is about not competing. And being around someone who does not need to prove themselves. Someone who is not faking calm, but has earned it through self-reflection, discipline, and emotional maturity.

Think about the people you naturally gravitate toward - the ones whose advice you actually listen to, whose presence feels calming, not chaotic.

Chances are they are not the one bragging about themselves. They're the ones who:

- *Speak with conviction but stay open to correction*
- *Admit when they don't know something - and mean it.*
- *Carry themselves like their life is not a performance, but a practice.*

That kind of presence can't be copied. It has to be cultivated. And the only way to cultivate it is through the inner work you've been doing so far - peeling back the layers, owning the patterns, setting your own standards.

Influence without grounding is manipulation waiting to happen. Confidence is rooted in clarity - not ego - people lean in.

Persuasion vs Manipulation

Manipulation operates through distortion - bending facts, playing on insecurities, leveraging fear or urgency to get a desired outcome. It's fast but it's fragile. People may follow for a while, but they'll remember how they felt under your influence. And if that feeling was pressure, guilt, or shame - you've lost them, even if they stayed silent.

Persuasion, however, is slow power. It builds trust, not tension. It aligns values, rather than exploiting vulnerabilities. When you persuade, you're not pulling people into your world, you're inviting them to step more fully into your world, with clarity and purpose. You help them see what's possible, not what they're missing.

At its best, persuasion is leadership. And leadership is service.

You're not trying to control the outcome. You're creating the conditions for insight, choice, and movement. The irony? This kind of influence is the most powerful - because it doesn't force. It frees.

If you're building social wealth, this matters. Because the world is full of short-term tacticians - people who game attention, exploit systems, or say what they think others want to hear. But long-term players - those who build reputational capital that compounds over decades - they play a different game.

They persuade through presence. They lead with integrity. And they win, not by taking more - but by becoming someone others want to follow.

> *Don't focus on being a person of success but rather focus on being a person of value.*

How to Intentionally Build Social Wealth

Most people know they should network, but few know how to do it without feeling fake, transactional, or exhausted. This section can break that down into simple, powerful practices:

1. **Show up consistently, not occasionally**
   People don't remember what you said. They remember how you made them feel. Being present regularly builds safety and reliability, especially in your middle and inner circles.

2. **Become a connector**
   Introduce people who can help each other. Don't wait for a reason - if you see alignment, make the intro. It cost nothing but builds social equity that always comes back.

3. **Listen more than you speak**
   People trust those who make them feel seen. In a world where everyone is trying to be interesting, be interested.

4. **Give without keeping score**
   The biggest networkers don't think in transactions. They operate from abundance. The moment your giving becomes conditional, it's no longer generous - it's manipulation.

5. **Keep weak ties warm**
   Comment on a post. Send a birthday message. Share something useful without asking for anything. It's not about big moves. It's about staying on the radar.

DO NOT

1. Ghost after asking for help
2. Taking more than you give - repeatedly
3. Forgetting name, birthdays, or basic context
4. Only reaching out when you need something
5. Failing to follow through on small commitments

6. Gossiping, bragging, or name-dropping excessively
7. Thinking visibility = value

Make Your Network Your Legacy

Social wealth is not just a career tool. It's a **life philosophy.**

One day, your career titles will fade. Your achievements will blur. Even your money may move into someone else's hands.

But the people you've helped? The doors you've opened? The young ones you mentored, the peers you backed, the values you stood for in every interaction - that's legacy.

The greatest networkers are not remembered for who they knew. They are remembered for how they made others feel.

Look at any city map and you'll see that property prices in one suburb can be triple those just a few kilometers away. On the surface, people assume it's because of the houses - the architecture, the square footage, the finishes. But buildings don't just make a suburb "rich". People do.

Wealth clusters because social wealth clusters.

Social wealth is not a tactic. It's a way of living. And the return? Compound trust. Unshakable influence. And the quiet power of knowing you did not rise alone - but when you do rise, you take others with you.

They change the course of entire families, communities, and industries. The connections you nurture today can become the opportunities, safety nets, and stepping stones for people you may never even meet. That's when social wealth stops being just personal capital… and becomes generational leverage.

Chapter 7: Do You See the Game Now?

The Board Was Always Rigged

Welcome to the game.
The sooner you stop expecting fairness, the sooner you can start winning.
You were born into a board that was already set.

The true game is not about money. Money is just a scoreboard. The game is about **influence, compliance,** and **control.**

- Who gets to decide what you think you need?
- Who controls the pace of your ambition.
- Who defines what “winning" even looks like.

The reason the game works so well is because humans are predictably irrational. Our brains run on shortcuts, biases, and emotional reflexes. We crave belonging, so we follow the crowd even when the crowd is running off the cliff. We fear loss more than we value gain, so we clutch at security even when it keeps us small. We chase instant rewards, so we sabotage the very futures we claim to want.

The people who built the board understand it better than you understand yourself. Every billboard, every price tag, every notification on your phone has been designed to pull one of your psychological levers. And if you can’t see the lever, you are the lever. If the product or service is free, you are probably the product.

You were never just playing the game. The game was playing you.

Mastering Your Four Triggers

Everything you've learned in this book - from rewiring your relationship with money, to building your financial identity, to cultivating social wealth - has been about breaking free from these exact **four triggers.**

1. Scarcity Triggers - Manufacturing Urgency

In The Poverty Mindset, we unpack how fear-based thinking locks you in survival mode. Scarcity triggers are the system's way of keeping you there - not by accident, but by design.

Your brain has a built-in loss aversion bias: losing $100 hurts roughly twice as much as gaining $100 feels good. The system exploits this imbalance. Scarcity doesn't just signal that something might run out - it hijacks your nervous system into believing your survival is at stake.

This is why scarcity messaging works even when you know it's fake:

- **Countdown timers** in online stores that magically reset the next day.
- "**Only two left in stock**" tags that appear on mass-produced products.

- **Breaking news headlines** designed to spike your cortisol before an ad break

Your rational brain might tell you, "I don't actually need this right now," but your survival brain hears, "If I don't act now, I lose. Permanently." And the survival brain moves faster than the rational one.

In the wild, scarcity kept us alive: if there were only a few fruit trees left in season, you had to act fast. In modern life, scarcity keeps us buying things we don't need, locking into deals we haven't researched, or panicking at market drops instead of sticking to a long-term plan.

When you learn to rewire your money mindset as covered earlier in this book, you were retraining your biology to pause, evaluate, and act from intention instead of impulse. That's the first step to neutralising scarcity triggers: slowing the game down so you can see the move before you make it.

2. Social Proof Loops - The Crowd as a Weapon

In Social Wealth & Networking Capital, we explored how proximity shapes opportunity. How being surrounded by the right people accelerates your growth.

Social proof loops exploit the other side of that truth: the same instinct that can lift you higher can also drag you straight into the fire.

Humans are wired to be tribal. For most of human history, survival depended on staying with the group. If the tribe ran, you ran - not because you knew why, but because falling behind could mean death. That wiring hasn't disappeared. The modern world simply swapped predators for trends, bubbles, and bad investments.

This is why "everyone is doing it" still works as a persuasion tactic:

- We see a product trending and assume it must be good.
- We see a stock price climbing and assume it must be safe to enter
- We see a crowd lining up for a restaurant and feel and urge to join them, even if we've never heard of the place.

Social proof bypasses logic and plugs directly into our need for belonging. If enough people are moving in one direction, we assume they know something we don't - even if they're just copying the person in front of them.

That's how bubbles form. That's how fads spread. That's how "meme stocks" go from obscure to explosive - and then collapse - in the span of weeks.

When you learned to build intentional networks earlier in the book, you were also learning to break this loop:

- To filter whose example you follow.
- To see whether the crowd's movement is based on insight or inertia.

- To have the courage to step sideways when everyone else is charging forward.

3. Identity Hijacking - Selling yourself

The most effective sales pitch is not about the product. It's about **who you believe you'll be once you own it.**

Marketers know that humans defend their self-image more fiercely than they defend their bank balance. This is why luxury brands don't really sell clothes, they sell the status of being seen in them. A rolex is not a timepiece; it's a wearable resume. A designer bag isn't just leather, it's a social password.

Fitness programs don't just sell workouts - they sell the identity of being fit. The before-and-after photos aren't really about health; they're about belonging to the tribe of the "after" picture.

Identity hijacking works because it taps into three primal needs:

1. Belonging - the need to be part of a group.
2. Significance - the need to feel important or respected.
3. Certainty - the need to feel that buying this thing will make you more of the person you want to be.

In Rewiring Your Financial Identity, we explored how your self-image quietly dictates your behaviour. If you see yourself as "bad with money," you unconsciously make decisions that reinforce that story. If you see yourself as an investor, you start behaving like one - even before you have the portfolio to match.

Marketers have learned to edit that story for you. They plant a gap between who you are now and who you could be, then position their product as the bridge. If you don't consciously design your own identity, the marketplace will do it for you - and it will almost always be in a way that keeps you buying.

How to master it:

- **Audit** the purchases you've made in the last year. Which were truly about utility - and which were about identity? Be brutally honest
- **Flip it**: Consciously design your "wealth identity" - the future self whose habits you want to live now. Filter every purchase through this lens. If it doesn't align, it doesn't enter your life.

4. Reward Manipulation - Training You Like a Lab Rat

In Emotional Debt, we explored how the nervous system can keep you trapped in reactive cycles - chasing relief, comfort, or stimulation in ways that sabotage your long-term goals. Reward manipulation is the same mechanism, but deliberately **weaponised**.

Your brain runs on dopamine - the chemical of anticipation and reward. It's not just released when you get something you want; it's released when you think you might get something. The system exploits this by creating endless loops of "almost there" moments that keep you hooked.

You see it everywhere:

- Gambling Mechanics in Finance Apps
  That mimics slot machines, making every trade feel like a spin you might win.

- Social Media Dopamine loops where likes, comments, and notification drip-feed validation.

- "Spend more to save more" - cashback traps that reward overspending with tiny rebates, making you feel like you're winning when you're actually losing.

These loops are designed to bypass logic entirely. They tap into the part of your brain that once kept our ancestors hunting and foraging - the part that says, keep going, the next reward could be the big one. The problem is, in the modern world, these rewards are often meaningless, and the cost is real.

When you learned emotional budgeting strategies earlier in this book, you were training to flip this lever in your favour. The goal isn't to eliminate rewards - it's to own the loop.

When you control your reward structures, you stop being trained like a lab rat - and start training yourself like an elite athlete.

How the System Studies You

These four psychological levers are the primary tools used in data blueprint to push your buttons. Every scroll, every second spent on watching a video, every like, every click - you are updating a behavioural profile so precisely, it can predict your next purchase before you even know you want it.

The modern economy runs on behavioural surveillance:

- Social media algorithms track how long your eyes linger on a post.
- E-commerce platforms know which price points make you hesitate and which make you click.
- Steaming services track the exact moment you stop watching so they can hook you faster next time.

And here's the unnerving part: it's not just about what you buy. It's about why you buy. Machine learning models analyse patterns you don't even notice in yourself - the time of day you're most impulsive, the colours that make you trust a brand, the headlines that trigger your curiosity or fear.

This is not a theory. Facebook once ran experiments tweaking the emotional tone of users' news feeds to see if they could make people happier or sadder. They could. And they did.

Think about that: the system can shift your mood before you've even realised it's changed - and then serve you offers, products, or investments optimised for that exact emotional state.

Without awareness, you are algorithmically predictable. And predictable people are profitable people.

Play the Game

The essence of dark psychology: Understanding the levers that have been used on you your entire life - and then flipping them to serve you instead of the system.

This book has given you a map - not just for wealth, but for growth, mindset, and self-mastery. Each checkpoint on that map has its own depth and complexity, far beyond what we can be contained in these pages. The deeper you go, the more you realise how vast the terrain really is. That's why the wisest players rarely speak loudly about the game - they've learned to move quietly and let things flow.

Your first move is emotional clarity. Read parenting books - not because you plan to raise children, but because they teach you the art of regulating emotions and staying composed under pressure. Journal your thoughts and feelings daily. Learn to name them. Then reframe them. Recognitive reframing isn't blind optimism - it's the discipline of understanding what's happening in your mind and choosing a perspective that keeps you in control. Nobody is coming to save you. You have to be the parent of your inner child.

Seek discomfort deliberately. Place yourself in situations that stretch your mental and emotional capacity. The more you practice this, the more rejection you'll face - and the more rejection you face, the quicker your brain will adapt. Comfort is a slow poison; it teaches you nothing but how to stand still.

Rejection and reframing will sting. They may tempt you to doubt yourself. This is where mindfulness matters. Never speak down to yourself. You are exactly where you're meant to be. This book isn't the conclusion - it's the beginning.

Sharpen your soft skills. Listen more than you speak. Practice rephrasing your words neutrally - real influence is passive. Study body language. Learn the tempo of the industry you want to enter. Keep asking questions. Keep learning. Keep refining.

Everything that you want or have is only temporary. If it's not yours, let it be. The only thing you can truly control is yourself.

Just Stop Being Poor is a refusal - a refusal to accept the script you were handed, the role you were assigned, and the limits someone else decided belonged to you.

P.S. Read the introduction again. It might hit you differently.

Made in United States
North Haven, CT
04 November 2026

21764041R00125